ASSESSING THE BASE FORCE

Studies in Defense Policy

SELECTED TITLES

STUDIES IN DEFENSE POLICY

ASSESSING THE BASE FORCE:
HOW MUCH IS TOO MUCH?

William W. Kaufmann

THE BROOKINGS INSTITUTION
Washington, D.C.

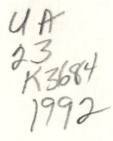

The paper used in this publication meets the minimum requirements of the
American National Standard for Information Sciences—Permanence of
Paper for Printed Library Materials, ANSI Z39.48-1984.

ⓑ THE BROOKINGS INSTITUTION

The Brookings Institution is an independent organization devoted to nonpartisan research, education, and publication in economics, government, foreign policy, and the social sciences generally. Its principal purposes are to aid in the development of sound public policies and to promote public understanding of issues of national importance.

The Institution was founded on December 8, 1927, to merge the activities of the Institute for Government Research, founded in 1916, the Institute of Economics, founded in 1922, and the Robert Brookings Graduate School of Economics and Government, founded in 1924.

The Board of Trustees is responsible for the general administration of the Institution, while the immediate direction of the policies, program, and staff is vested in the President, assisted by an advisory committee of the officers and staff. The by-laws of the Institution state: "It is the function of the Trustees to make possible the conduct of scientific research, and publication, under the most favorable conditions, and to safeguard the independence of the research staff in the pursuit of their studies and in the publication of the results of such studies. It is not a part of their function to determine, control, or influence the conduct of particular investigations or the conclusions reached."

The President bears final responsibility for the decision to publish a manuscript as a Brookings book. In reaching his judgment on the competence, accuracy, and objectivity of each study, the President is advised by the director of the appropriate research program and weighs the views of a panel of expert outside readers who report to him in confidence on the quality of the work. Publication of a work signifies that it is deemed a competent treatment worthy of public consideration but does not imply endorsement of conclusions or recommendations.

The Institution maintains its position of neutrality on issues of public policy in order to safeguard the intellectual freedom of the staff. Hence interpretations or conclusions in Brookings publications should be understood to be solely those of the authors and should not be attributed to the Institution, to its trustees, officers, or other staff members, or to the organizations that support its research.

FOREWORD

THE Defense Department began describing what became known as the base force in the summer of 1990. According to Secretary of Defense Richard B. Cheney, it was supposed to constitute a reduction of 25 percent from the cold war capabilities of the United States and reflect the revolutionary changes that had taken place in Eastern Europe and the Soviet Union.

In the fall of 1992, however, the Soviet Union no longer exists. Russia, the largest piece of it, is planning a defense establishment of no more than 1.5 million people. Presidents George W. Bush and Boris N. Yeltsin have agreed to reduce the American and Russian strategic nuclear arsenals to a maximum of 3,500 warheads on each side. The United States, at the head of a vast coalition, has dealt Iraq a stunning military defeat. General Colin L. Powell, chairman of the Joint Chiefs of Staff, has said that he is running out of enemies. Yet the dimensions of the base force have changed very little during the last two years. More than 1.6 million men and women will remain under arms. Between 1990 and 1997 the cost of the U.S. defense establishment will probably have fallen by just over 27 percent in real terms. By the year 2002, however, it is likely to have returned to today's level because of current plans that call for the procurement of major new and more sophisticated weapons during the next ten years.

In this study, William Kaufmann asks two basic questions: How plausible is the case for the base force? And what are the risks of substituting capabilities of substantially lower cost for what Secretary Cheney has described as the minimum capability essential for U.S. security?

To answer these questions, Kaufmann delineates the base force and the Defense Department's estimate of its cost. He then examines the formal justification for the proposed posture, with particular reference to the range of military challenges anticipated by its planners. Against this background, Kaufmann considers the contingencies used by the Pentagon for planning purposes and the U.S. forces required to defeat their hypothetical enemies. Finally, he analyzes the performance of smaller forces in the same contingencies and compares their effectiveness with that of the base force.

The study draws several conclusions from these comparisons. One is that the base force is an extremely conservative response to the expected international environment of the future. Moreover, as envisioned, that environment appears to be almost as dangerous as before the disintegration of the Soviet Union. Another conclusion is that even under the Pentagon's pessimistic assumptions, smaller forces could still achieve essentially the same results as the base force, but at a cost that would be lower by nearly 30 percent. Yet another conclusion is that a more aggressive U.S. and allied policy of dealing with such issues as weapons proliferation and regional tensions could lead to fewer contingencies and more modest but still highly capable forces, adequate to deal with residual threats and costing at least 40 percent less than the base force. Finally, Kaufmann suggests that a prudent program of reductions would aim to reach the goals of the first alternative force by fiscal 1997, and those of the second by fiscal 2002. Such a course of action, if followed to completion, would result in a cumulative saving over the ten-year period of more than $600 billion (in 1993 dollars).

William W. Kaufmann is a professor emeritus at the Massachusetts Institute of Technology and a nonresident senior fellow at Brookings, where he holds the Sydney Stein, Jr., Chair in International Security in the Foreign Policy Studies program. He is grateful to John D. Steinbruner for his comments on the manuscript. Tricia Dewey edited the manuscript, and Adrianne Goins verified its factual content. Susan Blanchard, Louise Skillings, Kirsten Soule, and Ann Ziegler typed the manuscript; and Charlotte B. Brady and Susanne Lane provided administrative supervision and support. Susan L. Woollen prepared the manuscript for typesetting.

Brookings is grateful for funding provided by the Carnegie Corporation of New York, the W. Alton Jones Foundation, Inc., and the John D. and Catherine T. MacArthur Foundation.

The views expressed in the study are those of the author and should not be ascribed to persons or organizations whose assistance is acknowledged, or to the trustees, officers, or other staff members of the Brookings Institution.

BRUCE K. MACLAURY
President

November 1992
Washington, D.C.

CONTENTS

TABLES

CHAPTER ONE

INTRODUCTION

In MARCH 1985, Mikhail S. Gorbachev inherited the leadership of the Union of Soviet Socialist Republics. Only a few months earlier, Congress had appropriated the largest defense budget in the peacetime history of the United States. In the more than seven years that followed, Gorbachev presided over and then fell victim to a revolution that brought about the freedom of Eastern Europe, the unification of Germany, the virtual collapse of Soviet military power, and the death of the USSR. In the United States, the defense budget went into a gradual decline, brought about less by the crumbling of the Soviet empire and the end of its foreign adventures than by a growing congressional concern over mounting federal deficits and increasingly evident problems in the U.S. economic and social structure.

Birth of the Base Force

Between fiscal 1985 and fiscal 1990, defense budget authority fell by 13 percent in real terms. More than 80 percent of the decline, however, came from reductions in the Defense Department's investments in procurement, research and development, and military construction (table 1-1). The size, composition, and readiness of the armed forces changed hardly at all. As much as 63 percent of defense budget authority continued to be allocated to the nuclear deterrence of the Soviet Union, the defense of Western Europe from attack by the countries of the Warsaw Pact, and the protection of sea lines of communication in the Atlantic, Mediterranean, and Pacific from Soviet attack submarines and aircraft (table 1-2).

1

Table 1-1. Defense Department Budget Authority, by Appropriation, Fiscal Years 1985–90
Billions of 1993 dollars unless otherwise specified

Appropriation	1985	1986	1987	1988	1989	1990	1985–90 reduction	Percent of total reduction
Military personnel	88.8	85.1	90.6	90.2	89.5	88.6	–0.2	a
Operations and maintenance	101.9	97.3	100.0	99.3	100.1	99.0	2.9	5.9
Procurement	126.8	117.7	98.6	94.7	90.5	89.7	37.1	75.6
Research, development, test, and evaluation	41.0	43.0	44.2	43.7	43.1	40.3	0.7	1.4
Military construction	7.2	6.8	6.3	6.4	6.6	5.7	1.5	3.1
Family housing	3.8	3.6	3.8	3.8	3.8	3.5	0.3	1.0
Other	6.1	5.6	2.2	0.5	0.2	–0.3	6.4	13.0
Total[b]	375.6	359.1	345.7	338.5	333.7	326.4	49.1	100.0

Sources: *Department of Defense Annual Report, Fiscal Year 1991*, p. 69; and *Department of Defense Annual Report, Fiscal Year 1993*, p. 131.
a. Less than 1 percent.
b. Numbers may not add to totals because of rounding.

Table 1-2. Annual Cost of Force Planning Contingencies, Fiscal Year 1990
Billions of 1993 dollars in budget authority

Force planning contingency	Cost
Strategic nuclear deterrence	49.7
Tactical nuclear deterrence	2.6
Non-nuclear defense of	
Northern Norway[a]	17.2
Central Europe	93.2
Mediterranean	7.8
Atlantic sea-lanes	22.4
Middle East and Persian Gulf	66.6
South Korea	19.6
Pacific sea-lanes	15.2
Alaska	1.4
Panama and Caribbean	3.3
Continental United States[b]	7.8
National intelligence and communications[c]	19.6
Total budget authority	326.4

Source: Author's estimates based on William W. Kaufmann and John D. Steinbruner, *Decisions for Defense: Prospects for a New Order* (Brookings, 1991), p. 39.
  a. Three carrier battle groups are assigned to this hypothetical operation.
  b. Consists of two carrier battle groups in overhaul and training.
  c. Does not include capabilities for tactical intelligence and communications.

Yet the rot in the Soviet empire was no longer possible for the Pentagon to ignore. By the early summer of 1990, as the defense budget and its advocates made their way around Capitol Hill, Secretary of Defense Richard B. Cheney responded to growing pressures from members of Congress by offering to reduce U.S. defenses by 25 percent—although he failed to define exactly what programs he would cut or what year he would use as the base from which to measure the reduction.[1] Shortly thereafter, what the Pentagon labeled the base force began to make its appearance in the media.[2]

Since then, plans for the base force have undergone some modification. The proposed strategic and tactical nuclear forces have shrunk dramatically. The programmed reduction in the much more expensive non-nuclear capabilities, on the other hand, has hardly changed at all. Even so, the estimated cost of what Cheney has characterized as the minimum capability required for the future security of the United States has gone down. In his most recent five-year defense program (FYDP), he has requested $267.6 billion in budget authority for fiscal 1993 and recommends reducing that total (in 1993 dollars) to $237.5 billion by fiscal 1997. These numbers reflect a cumulative cut of $47.4 billion from previously planned levels, brought about by the

Table 1-3. Defense Department Five-Year Defense Program, Fiscal Year 1993
Billions of 1993 dollars in budget authority

Item	1992	1993	1994	1995	1996	1997	Cumulative reduction, 1992–97
Fiscal 1992 FYDP	288.6	277.9	268.0	260.5	252.7	248.6	. . .
Adjusted summit level[a]	287.8	275.6	265.7	258.2	250.2	246.1	− 12.7
Program reductions	− 6.8	− 8.0	− 7.7	− 7.8	− 8.5	− 8.6	− 47.4
Fiscal 1993 FYDP	281.0[b]	267.6	258.0	250.4	241.8	237.5	− 60.2

Source: *Department of Defense Annual Report, Fiscal Year 1993*, p. 21, table 3a.

a. Defined as the January 1991 FYDP extended to 1997 and adjusted for 1991 congressional action, technical corrections, and revised inflation estimates.

b. Excludes incremental cost of Desert Shield and Desert Storm.

cancellation and deferral of major weapons programs (table 1-3). It is likely that Congress will reduce budget authority still further for fiscal 1993—by as much as 2.5 percent.

Magnitude of the Reductions

Secretary Cheney emphasizes the magnitude of the reductions he has proposed and uses a variety of measures to make his case. He points out that from fiscal 1985 to 1997, budget authority for the Defense Department will have declined, in real terms, by nearly 37 percent. He also notes that defense spending will fall from more than 6 to 3.4 percent of gross national product by fiscal 1997 (which assumes an annual rate of real growth in GNP of nearly 3 percent during the next five years), and that the defense share of federal spending will amount to only 16.3 percent. To demonstrate the change in relative budget priorities, he calculates that between fiscal 1985 and 1997, mandatory spending on such entitlements as social security will have increased by 33 percent and domestic discretionary spending, such as farm price supports, by 8 percent, while defense spending will have decreased by 26 percent—all in real terms. This last reduction, he argues, will take defense back almost to the levels that existed before the outbreak of the Korean War.[3]

There is, however, a different way to look at the budget reductions. If fiscal 1990 instead of 1985 is used as the base from which to measure

Table 1-4. Defense Department Budget Authority, Fiscal Years 1985–97
Billions of 1993 dollars

Year	Budget authority	Percent change	Year	Budget authority	Percent change
1985	375.6		1993	267.6	−7.02
1986	359.1	−4.39	1990–93	. . .	−18.01
1987	345.7	−3.73	1994	258.0	−3.59
1988	338.5	−2.08	1995	250.4	−2.95
1989	333.7	−1.42	1996	241.8	−3.43
1990	326.4[a]	−2.19	1997	237.5	−1.78
1985–90	. . .	−13.10	1990–97	. . .	−27.24
1991	292.9[a]	−10.26	1992–97	. . .	−17.48
1992	287.8[b]	−1.74			

Sources: Adapted from *Department of Defense Annual Report, Fiscal Year 1993*, pp. 22 (table 4), 131. See also tables 1-1 and 1-3.

a. Excludes cost of Desert Shield and Desert Storm.

b. The amount enacted in the fiscal 1992 Defense Department appropriation. See table 1-3 for the amended total for fiscal 1992 proposal in the new FYDP.

how much the end of the cold war has affected defense, it turns out that in real terms budget authority for the Pentagon will have fallen by 27.2 percent rather than 39 percent as of fiscal 1997 (table 1-4). The actual reduction over this seven-year period—$88.9 billion in real terms—would amount to a 46 percent cut in the resources devoted to the deterrence and containment of the USSR in fiscal 1990. As for the decline in defense as a percentage of GNP and federal outlays by fiscal 1997, these measures ignore the fact that in real terms both GNP and federal outlays will have grown much larger than they were in 1950. After all, 3.4 percent of $7 trillion yields a larger defense budget than 3.4 percent of $3 trillion.[4]

Perhaps more relevant in any event is a comparison of real spending for national defense at various times.[5] From the end of the Korean War to the outset of the Reagan administration (excluding the incremental costs of the war in Southeast Asia), the United States spent an average of $270 billion a year for national defense in 1993 dollars. During the eight years of the Reagan presidency, average annual outlays for national defense rose to $319 billion, an increase meant largely to overcome a series of alleged Soviet military advantages (table 1-5). By contrast, Secretary Cheney has proposed to wind down the cold war by spending $286 billion for national defense in fiscal 1993 and plans outlays of $250 billion by fiscal 1997. The total for 1993 is $6 billion more than the Reagan administration spent in fiscal 1982; the

Table 1-5. National Defense Outlays, Fiscal Years 1955–88
Billions of 1993 dollars

Year	Outlays	Year	Outlays
1955	300.0	1973	246.9
1956	284.3	1974	235.8
1957	288.7	1975	234.4
1958	282.3	1976	227.0
1959	283.6	1977	230.5
1960	276.9	1978	231.5
1961	277.8	1979	240.1
1962	292.0	1980	246.8
1963	296.2	1955–80 average annual	269.7
1964	292.2	1981	258.6
1965	264.3	1982	279.9
1966[a]	284.9	1983	303.5
1967[a]	284.9	1984	318.1
1968[a]	284.9	1985	342.3
1969[a]	284.9	1986	344.6
1970[a]	284.9	1987	356.5
1971[a]	284.9	1988	351.0
1972	272.0	1981–88 average annual	319.3

Source: Adapted from William W. Kaufmann, *Glasnost, Perestroika, and U.S. Defense Spending* (Brookings, 1990), table 1.
a. The incremental costs of the war in Southeast Asia are excluded.

Table 1-6. National Defense Program, Fiscal Years 1992–97
Billions of 1993 dollars

Item[a]	1992	1993	1994	1995	1996	1997
Budget authority						
Defense Department (051)	281.0	267.6	258.0	250.4	241.8	237.5
Energy Department and other	13.4	13.3	13.4	13.5	13.7	13.8
Total, national defense (050)	294.4	280.9	271.4	263.9	255.4	251.3
Outlays						
Defense Department (051)	293.0	272.8	257.6	248.4	242.1	236.5
Energy Department and other	13.1	13.1	13.1	13.1	13.3	13.4
Total, national defense (050)	306.1	285.9	270.7	261.5	255.4	249.9

Source: *Department of Defense Annual Report, Fiscal Year 1993*, p. 21, table 3.
a. The budget for national defense includes funds for the Department of Defense, the military applications of atomic energy (included in the budget of the Department of Energy), the strategic stockpile, and the selective service system. The functional classification of national defense is 050. The military activities of the Department of Defense are a subfunction of national defense and are classified as 051. The civil activities of the department are not included in either category.

outlays proposed for 1997 would still leave the total for national defense $3 billion higher than it was in fiscal 1980, after the Soviet invasion of Afghanistan and a renewed chill in the cold war (tables 1-5 and 1-6).

The Issue

However interesting these comparisons may be, the main issue is how much of the base force and its projected costs are really essential to maintain U.S. security in the emerging world order. To grapple with that issue it is necessary to understand what constitutes the base force, how it differs from the nuclear and non-nuclear U.S. capabilities deployed at the end of the cold war, and the nature of the case made by Secretary Cheney and his staff for this amount of military power. Only then does it become possible to consider alternatives to the base force and the range of choice that is possible in the years ahead.

Notes

1. William W. Kaufmann and John D. Steinbruner, *Decisions for Defense: Prospects for a New Order* (Brookings, 1991), p. 22.

2. Michael R. Gordon, "Pentagon Drafts Strategy for Post–Cold War World," *New York Times*, August 2, 1990, pp. A1, A14.

3. *Department of Defense Annual Report, Fiscal Year 1993*, pp. 1, 22–24; and *Budget of the United States Government, Fiscal Year 1993*, pt. 1, p. 36.

4. Ibid.

5. The budget for national defense includes funds for the Defense Department, the military applications of atomic energy appropriated to the Energy Department, the strategic stockpile, and the selective service system.

CHAPTER TWO

THE BASE FORCE

WHEN THE BASE force made its formal debut in early 1991, the USSR still led a precarious existence and Desert Shield had turned into Desert Storm. It is little wonder that, in the circumstances, Secretary of Defense Cheney insisted that the base force was "the minimum level necessary to protect U.S. interests and continue to play a leading role in shaping international events."[1]

Size of the Base Force

A great deal has happened since then, but the base force for the most part still stands firm, an apparently immovable object despite the seemingly irresistible forces of history. The defense budget will continue its annual real decline, at least until the end of fiscal 1997, according to current plans, although the principal elements of this "minimum" capability will be in place before then. Active-duty military personnel will fall from a recent peak of 2,174,000 in 1987 to 1,626,000 in 1997. In those same years, reserve forces personnel will supposedly shrink from 1,151,000 to 920,800 and civilian employees of the Defense Department from 1,133,000 to 904,000. The Army will suffer the most severe loss, with a 31 percent reduction from 781,000 in 1987 to 536,000 in 1995.[2]

Nuclear Forces

Of all the components of the base force, the strategic and tactical nuclear forces most clearly mirror the end of the U.S.-Soviet rivalry.

As late as fiscal 1990, the strategic offense was still a reflection of the cold war. It consisted of 1,000 intercontinental ballistic missiles (ICBMs), 584 submarine-launched ballistic missiles (SLBMs), and 244 heavy bombers, for a total of 1,828 launchers and, at first approximation, more than 12,300 nuclear warheads. By the end of fiscal 1992 (September 30, 1992), the total had fallen to 1,614 launchers and about 10,700 warheads.[3] For many years, the Strategic Air Command maintained 30 percent or more of its heavy bombers on runway alert with nuclear weapons on board, ready to take off within 15 minutes of an order; President Bush ended the alert. He also took the older Minuteman II ICBMs off alert, but continued to allow a high percentage of the SLBMs to hold stations within firing range of Russian targets. The 510 Minuteman III and 50 MX ICBMs also remained on alert.[4]

Once ratification and implementation of the START (strategic arms reduction talks) treaty are completed—by 1999 if not sooner—these forces would be reduced to 1,194 launchers. They would still be able to carry approximately 8,600 warheads, of which 6,000 would be accountable under the rules of the treaty. In his State of the Union message on January 28, 1992, President Bush proposed still further reductions, and President Boris Yeltsin of Russia responded with an offer to make even more dramatic cuts. When the two presidents met in Washington on June 17, 1992, they signed an accord that would ban all multiple independently targetable reentry vehicles (MIRVs) on land-based ballistic missiles (only one warhead per missile would be allowed), cut the number of warheads on 432 U.S. SLBMs—all of which are MIRVed—from approximately 3,456 to about 1,750, and placed a ceiling of 3,500 warheads (actual as well as accountable) on each country. The reductions to these new ceilings would take place in two stages and would be completed by the year 2003, or as early as 2000 if the United States assists Russia in the destruction of its nuclear weapons. Of course, launchers could be taken out of service and nuclear weapons put into storage and disabled in a much shorter period of time.[5]

In July 1992 President Bush also dealt with the related issues of nuclear weapons production and testing. On July 13 he announced as policy an end to the manufacture of weapons grade uranium and plutonium. In a letter to Congress three days earlier, the administration specified that the Energy Department would conduct no more than six nuclear tests a year, of which no more than three would exceed 35 kilotons in yield, and that the tests would be limited to insuring the safety and reliability of the existing arsenal. The United States, in actuality, had produced no U-235 for nuclear weapons since 1964 and had already suspended the production of plutonium in 1988. The limit on nuclear tests conformed with the program submitted to Congress some six months earlier for fiscal 1993.[6]

Despite all these changes, the United States will continue to press ahead with the deployment of a limited antiballistic missile defense and maintain land-based and space-based early warning systems as well as modest antibomber defenses. Encouraged by congressional passage of the Missile Defense Act of 1991, the Pentagon, after some internal dispute, has proposed an initial deployment of the global protection against limited strikes (GPALS) system that would comply with the antiballistic missile treaty. It would probably consist of a large radar and up to 100 interceptors located in Grand Forks, North Dakota, a site previously abandoned after the expenditure of approximately $14 billion (in 1993 dollars) on an earlier system. The Strategic Defense Initiative Organization estimates that the new site could be deployed by 1997 and would cost up to $18 billion.[7] Secretary Cheney, writing of the less demanding problem of air defense, has noted that it may not be possible to defend against improved cruise missiles launched from aircraft and submarines by upgrading current air defenses. And he has intimated that a more advanced air defense system would have to accompany the deployment of an antiballistic missile defense.[8] He did not discuss costs.

Tactical nuclear capabilities are already undergoing even more drastic cuts as the Red tide recedes. As a result of initiatives taken by President Bush in 1991, artillery-fired atomic projectiles and nuclear warheads for surface-to-surface missiles have been withdrawn from overseas and will be eliminated. All tactical nuclear weapons, including the Tomahawk cruise missiles with nuclear warheads, have been removed from U.S. surface ships, attack submarines, and land-based naval aircraft. According to Secretary Cheney, some of these weapons will be dismantled and destroyed; others will be placed in storage where they will be kept available for redeployment in the event of a crisis of undisclosed dimensions. Only nuclear aircraft munitions will be left overseas, mostly in Europe, to "serve as the link between conventional and strategic nuclear forces."[9]

Non-Nuclear Forces

The changes that will take place in U.S. non-nuclear forces by 1997 are not nearly as impressive. The Army, which had eighteen active and ten reserve divisions in 1990, is scheduled to lose six of the former and four of the latter by 1995. Active-duty personnel, which stood at 750,600 in 1990, will fall to 536,000 by 1995, a reduction of nearly 29 percent. The Marine Corps, which is required by law to maintain three divisions, will nonetheless give up two of its nine active-duty brigades as well as 32,000 of its regular military personnel. It will, however, retain its one reserve division. In sum, U.S. ground forces will shrink from thirty-two to twenty-two nominal divisions, a reduction of more than 31 percent.[10]

The Navy, in 1990, deployed a fleet of 508 battle force ships, not counting its 39 in the strategic nuclear forces (ballistic missile submarines and support ships). By 1997, it will lose 97 ships for a reduced battle force fleet of 411. Of that total, nearly 70 percent, or 284, will consist of aircraft carriers, surface combatants, nuclear attack submarines, and ships for amphibious operations. Active-duty personnel, at a strength of 583,000 in 1990, will decline to 501,000 by 1997, a drop of 14.1 percent—despite a reduction in the fleet of more than 20 percent.[11]

Even the fighter and attack aircraft of the Air Force, which performed such a stellar role in Desert Storm, will suffer wrenching cuts. In 1990, they formed the equivalent of approximately twenty-four active and twelve reserve wings, each with seventy-two combat plus support aircraft. By 1997, these two totals will fall to the equivalent of slightly more than fifteen active and eleven reserve fighter-attack wings. Current indications are, however, that the number of heavy bombers assigned to non-nuclear missions, currently at thirty-three, could easily double as more B-52s, and possibly the B-2s as well, are removed from the strategic nuclear forces. In any event, Air Force active-duty personnel (from the nuclear and airlift as well as the non-nuclear forces) will drop from 539,300 in fiscal 1990 to 430,000 in 1997, a decline of 20 percent.[12]

Strategic Mobility

Of the major non-nuclear components, only strategic mobility—or the capability of the armed forces to deploy overseas to critical areas in a timely fashion—is scheduled for increases. Actually, intercontinental airlift (including the Civil Reserve Air Fleet) will grow quite modestly, from 48 million to 53 million ton-miles a day as the new C-17 cargo aircraft, despite its many technical problems and cost overruns, replaces the C-141. Sealift, finally acknowledged as the backbone of strategic mobility, will increase in capacity by nearly 45 percent, from more than 830,000 short tons of equipment in a single sailing, to perhaps as many as 1.2 million short tons by the end of the decade. More than half the increased tonnage will come from the acquisition of twenty large, twenty-four-knot roll-on-roll-off ships, nine of which will be loaded with Army combat and combat support equipment. The remaining eleven will be fast sealift ships and will join the eight already on hand. Less noticed, but equally important, are the nearly 500,000 tons of matériel that remain pre-positioned in Europe (including Norway), the 275,000 tons stored in thirteen Maritime pre-positioning ships (for the Marines), and the twelve Afloat pre-positioning ships (for the Army, Navy, and Air Force), as well as the ability of the Civil Reserve Air Fleet (CRAF) to move nearly 20,000 people a day to a distant theater such as the Persian Gulf.[13]

What is most important about these numbers is what they imply for the movement of major ground and tactical air forces. According to Secretary Cheney, the programmed combination of pre-positioning, airlift, and sealift will give the Pentagon enough capacity to deploy to a theater outside Europe (such as the Persian Gulf or the Korean peninsula) a force of approximately five Army divisions, one Marine expeditionary force (MEF)—usually defined as a division and its accompanying air wing—and associated tactical fighter and naval forces, all in about eight weeks. For European contingencies, within about fifteen days, because of so much pre-positioned equipment, two Army divisions and perhaps five Air Force tactical fighter wings could reinforce the two Army divisions and associated fighter wings that are currently scheduled to remain in Europe. On the order of two Marine expeditionary brigades (MEBs) could also deploy to Norway in the same amount of time.[14]

Power and Effectiveness

It is quite probable that, while the base force is considerably smaller in numbers than the 1990 capabilities, it is only slightly lower in combat power and effectiveness. Many of the Navy's ships and the Air Force's tactical aircraft were approaching obsolescence, and neither of the services would have had the resources to replace all of them with modern equipment. Cutbacks, in other words, were only a matter of time. Meanwhile, the older units did not add all that much to the performance of the forces. Other factors have mitigated the effects of the cuts as well. Because Russian nuclear and non-nuclear forces are undergoing a major contraction, the number of targets that the U.S. strategic offense might be called on to cover should also fall, along with the number of U.S. launchers and warheads. None of these reductions in nuclear weapons would make deterrence any less effective than it was at the height of the cold war.

Non-nuclear warfare is influenced by spatial considerations in a way that would probably not be the case in strategic nuclear exchanges. Consequently, reductions in U.S. non-nuclear forces are bound to be constrained by the geography of the theaters to which they might be committed and by the need to create barriers to attack whether on land, at sea, or in the air. But neither an Arabian nor a Korean theater of operations would make the kind of demands for force density levied by the central region of Europe at the height of the cold war, when the assumption of a massive ground and air attack by the Warsaw Pact constituted the key non-nuclear planning contingency.

Modernization

What is more, the United States will be able to deploy forces that will have, by any standard, very modern equipment for some years to come. During the last two decades, the Pentagon has purchased at least $57 billion (in 1993 dollars) worth of tanks, other combat vehicles, and helicopters for the Army; the Navy has acquired $224 billion in aircraft carriers, attack submarines, surface combatants, and combat aircraft; and the Air Force has spent $84 billion just on 1,044 F-15 and 2,189 F-16 fighters.[15] No potential adversary currently on the horizon will have anything comparable to the base force in combat power, effectiveness, strategic reach, and tactical mobility. In fact, one of the ironies of the base force is that it will have more strength than it can deploy under some of the conditions foreseen by the force planners of the Joint Staff (a body now under the direction of General Colin L. Powell).

Secretary Cheney, recognizing that previous acquisition policies in the 1980s had produced major quantities of modern weaponry intended for capabilities larger than the base force, has reduced the Pentagon's procurement budget by a substantial amount. Budget authority for procurement in fiscal 1985 came to $126.8 billion in 1993 dollars; Cheney requested only $54.4 billion for the same purposes in fiscal 1993. This was a 57 percent cut from 1985, a drop of 45 percent from 1987, and a reduction of more than 39 percent from 1990.[16]

To achieve these reductions, Secretary Cheney has terminated a number of programs. The strategic nuclear forces have had to abandon all plans for future modernization: B-2 bomber production will halt at twenty aircraft, and construction of Tridents will stop at eighteen submarines, while the rail garrison MX and the small ICBM will not even be produced. The non-nuclear forces will have to go without further M-1 Abrams tanks and Bradley fighting vehicles, AH-64 Apache attack helicopters and SSN-21 advanced attack submarines, and F-14, F-15, and F-16 combat aircraft. The services will be living for the most part with existing inventories of these and other weapons for some years to come.[17]

This seemingly draconian policy is not as impressive as it sounds. The list of cuts is long, but the list of candidates for deletion is even longer. Despite that, the Defense Department is not about to abandon the business of major weapons acquisition if Cheney has his way. The secretary favors vigorous research and development, the prototyping of new systems, the avoidance of concurrent deployment and testing of advanced systems (flying before buying, as the saying goes), and selected procurement. To implement this policy, he plans to start the production of fourteen major new systems or subsystems during the next five years. They include such expensive items as the F-22 stealth fighter, the joint surveillance target and attack radar aircraft (JSTARS), a stretched version of the F/A-18 aircraft, a variety of advanced munitions, and new communications satellites. Yet another nuclear-powered aircraft carrier is to be built and completed by the end of the century, and more guided missile destroyers of the DDG-51 class will be added to the battle forces of the Navy.[18] Secretary Cheney also seems to favor the early deployment of a limited ABM defense, even though it will entail concurrent testing of the system's interceptors.[19]

This combination of new initiatives and familiar programs suggests that by the end of the 1990s it will become increasingly difficult to maintain the base force, major new procurement, and the budget constraint projected by Cheney. Indeed, there is a distinct possibility that, under current plans, the cost of defense will begin to grow again, by as much as 2 percent a year in real terms, as early as 1997.[20] Something will almost certainly have to give. Since the budgeting constraint is unlikely to be removed, decisions will have to be made on the rationing of declining resources between forces and modernization. The sooner these decisions are made, the fewer the resources that will be wasted on capabilities that subsequently have to be discarded. All the more reason, therefore, to see how much of the base force can be justified.

Notes

1. *Department of Defense Annual Report, Fiscal Year 1992*, p. 4.

2. William W. Kaufmann and John D. Steinbruner, *Decisions for Defense: Prospects for a New Order* (Brookings, 1991), p. 29, table 5-1; and *Department of Defense Annual Report, Fiscal Year 1993*, p. 25.

3. *Department of Defense Annual Report, Fiscal Year 1993*, pp. 60, 137.

4. Ibid., pp. 59–60.

5. Ibid., p. 60; and "Bush and Yeltsin Arms Cuts: Positive Steps to End the Arms Race," Council for a Livable World, Washington, June 17, 1992.

6. Michael R. Gordon, "It's Official: U.S. Stops Making Material for Nuclear Warheads," *New York Times*, July 14, 1992, p. A18; and Dunbar Lockwood, "Bush Declares New Testing Limits; Few Changes Actually Planned," *Arms Control Today*, vol. 22 (July–August 1992), p. 26.

7. R. Jeffrey Smith, "SDI Adopts 'High Risk' Procurement," *Washington Post*, July 3, 1992, p. A6.

8. *Department of Defense Annual Report, Fiscal Year 1993*, pp. 66–67.

9. Ibid., p. 65.

10. Ibid., pp. 69, 135, 138; "Manpower," table distributed by the Department of Defense, n.d.; and Kaufmann and Steinbruner, *Decisions for Defense*, p. 29.

11. *Department of Defense Annual Report, Fiscal Year 1993*, pp. 75–76, 135; "Manpower," table distributed by DOD; and Kaufmann and Steinbruner, *Decisions for Defense*, p. 29.

12. *Department of Defense Annual Report, Fiscal Year 1993*, pp. 80–81, 135, 138; Kaufmann and Steinbruner, *Decisions for Defense*, p. 29; and "Manpower," table distributed by DOD.

13. *Department of Defense Annual Report, Fiscal Year 1993*, pp. 94–97; *Department of Defense Annual Report, Fiscal Year 1992*, pp. 78–79; and "Sealift Program Finally Launched," *Armed Forces Journal International*, vol. 129 (March 1992), p. 11.

14. *Department of Defense Annual Report, Fiscal Year 1993*, pp. 97–98; and *Department of Defense Annual Report, Fiscal Year 1992*, pp. 78–79.

15. Raymond J. Hall, "Total Quantities and Costs of Major Weapon Systems Procured, FY1974-1993," Congressional Budget Office, March 18, 1991, pp. 27–56.

16. See table 1-1; and *Department of Defense Annual Report, Fiscal Year 1993*, p. 131.

17. *Department of Defense Annual Report, Fiscal Year 1992*, p. 26, and *Department of Defense Annual Report, Fiscal Year 1993*, p. 25; Joint Chiefs of Staff, *1992 Joint Military Net Assessment* (Secretary of Defense, August 21, 1992/Unclassified Version), p. 5-5; and Raymond J. Hall, "Selected Weapons Costs from the President's 1993 Program," Congressional Budget Office, May 1992, p. A-7.

18. John Lancaster, "White House Outlines Vision of New Military," *Washington Post*, January 30, 1992, p. A10; and "Major Systems in the FY1993 Budget," chart distributed by the Department of Defense, n.d.

19. Smith, "SDI Adopts 'High Risk' Procurement," p. A6.

20. Author's estimates based on four staff memoranda from the Congressional Budget Office, Washington, December 1991: "Fiscal Implications of the Administration's Proposed Base Force";"The Costs of the Administration's Plan for the Air Force through the Year 2010"; "The Costs of the Administration's Plan for the Army through the Year 2010"; and "The Costs of the Administration's Plan for the Navy through the Year 2010."

CHAPTER THREE

THE CASE FOR THE BASE FORCE

LEGEND HAS IT THAT when Gypsy Rose Lee, the famed ecdysiast, traveled from Broadway to Hollywood she brought with her a wardrobe of twelve empty trunks. Whether the base force is accompanied by weightier intellectual baggage is matter for conjecture.

Both President Bush and Secretary Cheney have acknowledged that the new world order differs from the old one in several important respects. But Cheney, as the principal spokesman for defense, has not found it easy to explain why the most important components of the base force have remained fixed after two more years of startling change.

The Old Strategy

The rivalry between the Soviet Union and the United States certainly dominated the old world order, but not to the exclusion of everything else. Cheney alleges that the central planning assumption of the previous era was that U.S. forces must be prepared to fight a global war stemming from a surprise attack by the Warsaw Pact in Europe. The actuality, however, was that U.S. planning for much of the cold war allowed for the possibility not only of a nuclear exchange escalating from aggression in Central Europe but also of regional conflicts such as those in Korea and Southeast Asia. Such was the basis for the misnamed 2½-war and 1½-war strategies of the 1960s and 1970s (discussed further in chapter 4). Yet despite the liberation of Eastern Europe, the unification of Germany, the collapse of the Soviet Union, and the new relationship with Russia, Cheney argues that "as the international security environment becomes more complex, so too do the requirements of national defense."[1]

Cheney argues that the "new," regionally focused defense strategy and the base force to implement it were not simply a scaling back of the ideas and capabilities he had inherited from the cold war. According to him, the new strategy "and the Base Force to implement it were built by judging what would be needed to further democracy and our national security interests in a post–Cold War world. We took a completely fresh look at our defense requirements rather than just building a smaller version of the Cold War military."[2]

Strategic Depth

Secretary Cheney, as a result of this review, has advanced a concept he calls strategic depth. This notion acknowledges that threats to U.S. security have become more distant not only physically but also in time. In fact, according to the secretary, the country faces no adversary capable of making a global challenge, although Russian strategic nuclear forces must remain a source of concern. As he points out, no power matches the United States in non-nuclear military technology or in the application of technology to weapons and tactics.[3]

The secretary claims that the United States lacked strategic depth during the cold war. Policymakers and planners, according to this view, could anticipate only one or two weeks of warning and response time before an attack by the Warsaw Pact in Europe—an attack that could drive the United States to the brink of a nuclear exchange. In the new world order, by contrast, an adversary intent on challenging U.S. and allied interests would face the hurdles of a united opposition and the qualitative advantages demonstrated against Iraq in Desert Storm. As a consequence, the United States now commands sufficient strategic depth to respond in a graduated manner to an attack and to preclude the domination of critical regions by hostile nondemocratic aggressors. President Bush has identified those regions as Europe, the Pacific, the Mediterranean, and the Persian Gulf.[4]

The Need for Strategic Offensive Forces

Cheney does not try to make any connection between strategic depth and the evolution of the U.S. strategic nuclear forces. That is no doubt in part because these forces have become so much the province of the White House and the process of arms reduction. But both he and the president emphasize the threat of proliferation that hangs over the new world order. President Bush, two years ago, noted that "right now, 20 countries have the capacity to produce chemical weapons. And by the year 2000, as many as 15 developing nations could have their own ballistic missiles. In the future, even conflicts we once thought of as limited or local may carry far-reaching consequences."[5] Cheney added an even more somber note early in 1991: "By the year 2000, it is estimated that at least 15 developing nations will have the ability to build ballistic missiles—8 of which either have, or are near to acquiring, nuclear capabilities. Thirty countries will have chemical weapons, and 10 will be able to deploy biological weapons as well." He also remarked that "while the threat to the U.S. homeland from such systems is minimal today, within the decade the continental United States could be in the range of the ballistic missiles of several Third World nations in a world dominated by multipolar geopolitical considerations, rather than the East-West strategic paradigms of the past 40 years."[6] By 1992, Cheney's prognosis had grown even worse. The number of developing nations estimated to have a capacity for biological and chemical weapons by the end of the decade remained the same as in 1991, but those that could acquire ballistic missiles through overt or covert channels shot up to twenty or more, and the nuclear proliferators rose to as many as nine.[7]

The secretary responded to these prospects by noting that "even as emphasis shifts from global war to regional conflicts, strategic nuclear deterrence remains a fundamental element of the U.S. defense strategy." He concluded that "while U.S. strategy has traditionally focused on deterring a unitary, rational actor with full knowledge and respect for the consequences of nuclear war, it must now also encompass potential instabilities that could arise when states or leaders perceive they have little to lose from employing weapons of mass destruction."[8]

A draft of the Defense Planning Guidance (DPG), which seems to have been repudiated after portions of it were leaked to the press, proposed a three-pronged strategy to deal with the "unitary, rational actor" and the irrational "states or leaders." Because Russia will remain "the only power in the world with the capability of destroying the United States," planners must continue to target vital aspects of the former Soviet military establishment and "hold at risk those assets and capabilities that current—and future—Russian leaders or other nuclear adversaries value most."[9]

Beyond that, "the actual use of weapons of mass destruction," by reckless leaders such as Saddam Hussein of Iraq, "even in conflicts that otherwise do not directly engage U.S. interests, could spur further proliferation which in turn would threaten world order." The United States thus could "be faced with the question of whether to take military steps to prevent the development or use of weapons of mass destruction." Such steps, according to the draft DPG, could include preemption of an impending attack. Alternatively, the United States might wait until after the attack to retaliate or threaten to punish aggressors by a variety of means, including strikes against the plants making weapons of mass destruction.[10]

The draft DPG also pointed to another problem that could further complicate decisions about nuclear targets and forces. The nonproliferation treaty of 1968 will come up for renewal in 1995. Suppose that the bid for an extension of the treaty were then to fail. According to the draft, "there could ensue a potentially radical destabilizing process" that could produce "critical challenges which the U.S. and concerned partners must be prepared to address."[11] One implication of this and other threats is that planners will have to develop a long and varied target list to cover all the contingencies and a substantial offensive force to ensure an acceptable probability of destruction against the designated aiming points.

The Need for Strategic Defenses

There is another implication of the threat postulated by the draft DPG. If the offensive forces could provide the options of preemption and retaliation—and thereby deter that unitary, rational actor—there remain those states or leaders with long-range ballistic missiles, nuclear warheads, and supposedly little to lose. According to the draft DPG, even Russia might fall into this category, because the possibility would remain of "robust strategic nuclear forces in the hands of those who might revert to closed, authoritarian, and hostile regimes."[12] Secretary Cheney has also argued, in a somewhat contrary fashion, that "measures that sufficed to answer the Soviet threat are no longer adequate in the face of the wide array of potential contingencies confronting the United States," not only in the next decade but today as well.[13]

Because of these dangers, the Defense Department, in Cheney's words, "has embarked on an aggressive program of strategic defense—centered on the Global Protection Against Limited Strikes (GPALS) system—to protect U.S. troops in the field and our allies from tactical ballistic missile attack, and to protect the United States itself from a ballistic missile attack."[14] President Bush, nearly two years earlier, had expressed equal confidence in what was to become GPALS. He was convinced, he said, that a defensive strategic deterrent made more sense in the 1990s than ever before. What better means of defense was there, he asked, "than a system that destroys only missiles launched against [the United States] without threatening a single life?"[15] He did not mention cost, performance, or the possibility that retaliation, resulting in many lives lost, might prove necessary to discourage other potential attackers from testing the effectiveness of GPALS. After all, tyrants might be just as capable of such acts as of other possible follies.

Non-Nuclear Needs

If strategic depth had nothing to do with nuclear issues, it presumably was one of the foundations of the new non-nuclear strategy. To defend this depth, the United States would need to maintain a forward presence overseas, the capabilities for a sustained response to a crisis, and the basis for reconstituting much larger forces. Such a strategy, Cheney argued, would "preclude potential aggressors from initiating regional arms races, raising regional tensions, or dominating critical regions."[16]

The original draft of the DPG elaborated on this theme by proposing to "prevent the re-emergence of a new rival, either on the territory of the former Soviet Union or elsewhere, that poses a threat on the order of that posed formerly by the Soviet Union."[17] To this end, the United States "must sufficiently account for the interests of the advanced industrial nations to discourage them from challenging our leadership or seeking to overturn the established political and economic order." The United States must also "maintain the mechanisms for deterring potential competitors from even aspiring to a larger regional or global role." Since those to be discouraged were not only Russia, Iraq, Iran, North Korea, and Cuba, but also apparently Germany, Japan, and

India, large, if unspecified, military capabilities would obviously be required.[18]

According to the discarded version of the DPG, none of this meant that the United States would or could become the world's policeman responsible "for righting every wrong." It did mean, however, that "we will retain the pre-eminent responsibility for addressing selectively those wrongs which threaten not only our interests, but those of our allies or friends, or which could seriously unsettle international relations."[19] The lone superpower would pick and choose its high noons.

Much of the hotter rhetoric about the necessity for U.S. leadership and the actions required to maintain it has apparently been abandoned in favor of support for the United Nations and collective action. Even so, Secretary Cheney, while strong in his emphasis on strategic depth and its contribution to these policies, seems to surrender it in order to advance the case for the base force. Victory in the cold war may have bought time and the opportunities for coalition building, yet the secretary also suggests "that nondemocratic powers might attempt to achieve hegemony in regions that remain critical to U.S. interests, and that such threats could arise with little or no warning." Indeed, threats to U.S. "vital interests could arise with little notice in various parts of the world, including Europe, Asia, Southwest Asia, and Latin America."[20]

Forward presence as a determinant of force size and composition also seems forgotten. Cheney emphasizes how crucial it is, but goes on to say—despite the dangers of sudden attacks—that the reduced threat and the accomplishments of arms control permit a considerable reduction in overseas deployments. Troop strength in Europe is to be cut roughly in half (to perhaps 150,000) by 1995, and more than 25,000 men and women will be taken out of East Asia, including the Philippines, by the end of 1992. Additional forces were to be withdrawn from South Korea, but plans to do so have been suspended pending further knowledge about the status of the North Korean nuclear program.[21]

Even the need to prepare for the reconstitution of the forces of the cold war no longer seems of much consequence. Cheney says he still considers it an important element in the new regional strategy. But, in a convenient revival of strategic depth, he reminds his audiences that "the Soviet Union has ceased to exist," that "military forces in the former Soviet Union have been cut even further" than was anticipated when reconstitution was first introduced, and that "the length of time that would be required for Russia, or any other potential adversary, to mount . . . a challenge is increasing."[22] Better still, "arms control agreements have supported our national security policy by channeling force postures in more stabilizing directions, by injecting greater predictability and transparency into military relationships, and by reducing force levels in ways that enhance the national security of the United States and its allies and negotiating partners."[23] In other words, arms control and reduction can reduce uncertainty and the need for reconstitution. Presumably this other route to national security can also substitute to some degree for a crisis response capability, but Cheney does not volunteer such a possibility.

Strategy and Force Planning

This is not to suggest that forward presence, crisis response, and reconstitution are lacking in relevance to U.S. security, with or without strategic depth. What should be evident, however, is that strategies such as the one propounded by President Bush and Secretary Cheney give no specific guidance to the kind of force size and composition the United States should maintain. Consequently, these "strategies" are not persuasive as explanations for the general, much less the specific, dimensions of the base force. In fact, despite the rhetoric of President Bush's national security strategy, Secretary Cheney's annual report to Congress, and drafts of the DPG, the United States is incapable of implementing a grand military strategy in any traditional sense. Americans have no interest in conquering the world and little interest in running it. The military initiative lies in someone else's hands.

The upshot is that force planners must ply their trade in the face of considerable but not infinite uncertainty. This is nothing new. Force planning has had to cope with this uncertainty for many years. Thus far, the development of hypothetical but plausible contingencies is the only known way to permit the design and testing of such structures as the base force and possible alternatives to it.

General Powell, who has a talent for avoiding such arcane terms as *unitary actors* and *hegemons*, knows how to cut through the rhetoric and articulate this simple truth. As he pointed out in testimony to

Congress, "we considered the *potential threats* to US interests around the world. While we recognize that we cannot predict the exact location and nature of future threats, we have developed planning scenarios that focus on regions where US vital interests are likely to be threatened." Although he did not describe the results of this process, he concluded "that the United States must retain certain *capabilities* to protect its interests around the globe. These include maritime and aerospace superiority, strategic agility, power projection, technological superiority and decisive force." He also warned Congress that "with the international political situation as unsettled as it is today, it would be imprudent to make massive cuts too quickly."[24]

New Perspectives

Of General Powell's conclusions, two are particularly striking. The first is that "we have shifted our planning focus from a single monolithic global scenario to an array of regional scenarios—similar to the type we experienced in confronting Iraq in the Gulf."[25] His allusions to potential threats and regional scenarios suggest that, rhetoric aside, the base force is firmly rooted in a thirty-year tradition of force planning contingencies and their implications.

The second conclusion lies in his reference to "decisive force." What he seems to be saying is that with the end of the cold war the United States need no longer fear the entry of the Soviet Union on the side of an enemy followed by a possible clash of two superpowers armed to the teeth with nuclear weapons, a nightmare that has haunted presidents for decades. Because the Soviet Union has disintegrated and Russia has moved to the sidelines, the United States is now free, as it never was during the cold war, to defeat an enemy—as it did Iraq—by the application of decisive force.

A revised version of the draft DPG has gone beyond General Powell's public statement. It directs the military services to prepare for the simultaneous occurrence of two major regional conflicts. At the same time they should plan to maintain a sizable U.S. military presence in Europe. The newer draft also makes a specific commitment to the security of Israel and the provision of modern military equipment to Taiwan.[26]

There is nothing particularly startling about these commitments. Furthermore, commitments by themselves, whether formal or informal, explicit or implicit, are not what determine the size and composition of U.S. forces. Rather, as General Powell has indicated, the main threats to U.S. interests—whether they be territorial or psychological— and the number of simultaneous attacks deemed plausible by U.S. policymakers are what should (parochial considerations aside) shape the nature of the military establishment and the weight of the defense budget. It is true, in this connection, that during the cold war more than 60 percent of the defense budget went to deterring and containing the Soviet Union. It is not necessarily true, however, that with the demise of the Soviet Union and its empire, the United States should maintain a defense capability that costs only 37 percent of what it did in 1990. The Soviet empire may have died, but as the Pentagon is quick to stress, Russia still exists, controls at least the facade of a large nuclear capability, and could revert to its bad old ways, admittedly after a matter of years. Furthermore, it can still be argued, as Secretary Cheney has done, that other regional dangers have become more menacing. And although General Powell has not made a great deal of it in public, his emphasis on the decisive use of force certainly implies that the size and composition of the non-nuclear capabilities will have to be larger for a given contingency than they were in the years when the planning objective was a forward defense, whatever the theater of operations, and the ability to sustain the defense for a limited period of time. But whether the Defense Department, in its consideration of various contingencies, has made the case for reducing real defense budgets by no more than 27 percent (from 1990 to 1997) is quite another matter.

Notes

1. *Department of Defense Annual Report, Fiscal Year 1993*, p. 59.

2. *Department of Defense Annual Report, Fiscal Year 1993*, p. 1. See also George Bush, "In Defense of Defense," speech to the Aspen Institute Symposium, August 2, 1990, reprinted as appendix E in *Department of Defense Annual Report, Fiscal Year 1992*, pp. 131–34.

3. *Department of Defense Annual Report, Fiscal Year 1993*, p. 2.

4. Bush, "In Defense of Defense," p. 132.

5. Ibid., p. 133.

6. *Department of Defense Annual Report, Fiscal Year 1992*, pp. ix–x, 59.

7. *Department of Defense Annual Report, Fiscal Year 1993*, pp. vi, 65.

8. Ibid., p. 59.

9. Patrick E. Tyler, "U.S. Strategy Plan Calls for Insuring No Rivals Develop," *New York Times*, March 8, 1992, p. 14. Quotations are from the draft DPG.

10. Ibid.

11. Ibid.

12. Ibid.

13. *Department of Defense Annual Report, Fiscal Year 1993*, p. 59.

14. Ibid.

15. Bush, "In Defense of Defense," p. 132.

16. *Department of Defense Annual Report, Fiscal Year 1993*, p. 2.

17. "Excerpts from Pentagon's Plan: 'Prevent the Re-Emergence of a New Rival,'" *New York Times*, March 8, 1992, p. 14.

18. Tyler, "U.S. Strategy Plan," pp. 1, 14. Quotations are from the draft DPG.

19. "Excerpts From Pentagon's Plan."

20. *Department of Defense Annual Report, Fiscal Year 1993*, p. 6.

21. Ibid., p. 8.

22. Ibid., p. 9.

23. Ibid., p. 10.

24. Statement of General Colin L. Powell, Chairman of the Joint Chiefs of Staff, before the Senate Committee on Armed Services, January 31, 1992, pp. 9–10 (emphasis in original).

25. Ibid., p. 5.

26. Patrick E. Tyler, "Pentagon Drops Goal of Blocking New Superpowers," *New York Times*, May 24, 1992, p. 1.

CHAPTER FOUR

CONTINGENCIES AND FORCE PLANNING

EXACTLY WHY THE identification of particular contingencies and their analysis are important to force planning deserves some repetition of the obvious. Defense leaders cannot ask Congress for a blank check with which to buy unspecified capabilities. Nor can they argue persuasively that uncertainty about the future is so great that they must prepare for every conceivable contingency and fortify the moon. Resources, after all, are limited, and the demand for them always exceeds the supply. In any event, military endeavors, like other activities, run into diminishing returns to scale.

As a consequence of these constraints, force planners must take out hedges against uncertainty by buying the capabilities to cope with one or more specific and plausible contingencies. They must also attempt to measure the performance of these capabilities and show what it will cost to buy differing levels of effectiveness. Only then can the national leadership make a reasonable determination about objectives, forces, budgets, and risks.

Steps in Force Planning

The process of force planning must obviously begin by identifying the neighborhoods, as General Powell describes them, in which aggression may occur. But that is only a first step. To go from the general to the specific, planners must comb neighborhoods for realistic attackers and develop feasible scenarios of what potential enemies might do. Once attacking forces and plans have been laid out, planners are then able to determine what role, if any, U.S. allies might play in resisting the attack. With that settled, they can proceed to test the performance of various U.S. contributions to the achievement of such military objectives as the destruction of targets, a sustained forward defense of friendly territory, or the annihilation of the enemy's forces. Finally, how the United States should respond to some combination of nuclear and non-nuclear contingencies will, at least in principle, determine U.S. force size and composition.

Traditional Contingencies

In the past, force planners have devoted the most attention to four major contingencies. The key nuclear contingency for their purposes has been a Soviet attack, delivered with minimum warning, designed to destroy U.S. retaliatory forces. The largest non-nuclear contingency has been an attack on Central Europe by the Warsaw Pact launched by as many as ninety divisions with only two weeks of warning. This contingency could also include the invasion of northern Norway, Greece, and Turkey. The other two planning contingencies have consisted of a Soviet effort to overrun Iran and a North Korean attack on South Korea. Planners have also considered the implications for the United States of Chinese attempts to invade Taiwan, Southeast Asia, and northern India.

In the 1960s, when both the Soviet Union and China were seen as possible belligerents, some planners argued that the United States should have sufficient forces to respond to simultaneous attacks from all around the Sino-Soviet bloc. Added up, these forces would have run to more than fifty divisions and an even larger number of fighter-attack wings. Secretary of Defense Robert S. McNamara, however, took the position that neither the Soviet Union nor China had the resources to fight on more than one front at a time, though he did agree that another country such as Cuba might take advantage of such a situation to cause trouble on its own.[1]

Strategy in the 1960s

This evaluation led to what became known as the 2½-war strategy, at best a misnomer of the number of contingencies then being used to derive U.S. force size and composition. Not only did the nuclear

surprise attack contingency shape the size of the U.S. retaliatory forces; it also led to debates about appropriate targets in the Soviet Union and the desirability of major antiballistic missile and antibomber defenses as well as a program of fallout shelters to limit damage in the event of a nuclear exchange.[2] Threats in Europe, Korea, and Cuba were the main basis for ground and tactical air forces. But the elusive issue of how to incorporate non-nuclear forces of the Navy into this kind of planning remained only partially resolved, much to the satisfaction of that semisovereign service.

McNamara was the first to admit that the use of contingencies to hedge against uncertainty did not constitute a prediction. In his view, indeed, events were unlikely to turn out as he and the force planners had imagined, especially if deterrence worked. But he also maintained that if U.S. forces, in conjunction with allies, could cope with the most threatening and testing contingencies, they should suffice to deal with the other, unexpected challenges that might arise.[3] His gamble, in effect, was that two simultaneous contingencies of major proportions would constitute the worst eventuality to confront the United States in the foreseeable future. Should an even more disastrous series of aggressions occur, however—along the lines of the "worldwide" war allegedly imagined by force planners during the Reagan administration—the areas considered most vital to U.S. security could at the very least be defended. Others could be liberated at a later date.

Strategy in the 1970s and 1980s

Another less conservative strategy could have been chosen with striking implications for the size of the forces and the defense budget. The Nixon, Ford, and Carter administrations actually did choose such a strategy. All three were willing to settle for the strategic nuclear deterrent and sufficient non-nuclear capabilities to deal with one major and one minor contingency. The collapse of the Sino-Soviet bloc and the increasingly hollow threat to use nuclear weapons if enemies overstretched U.S. and allied non-nuclear forces were the alleged reasons for the 1½-war strategy. What is more, even the Reagan administration, despite its rhetoric about Soviet across-the-board superiority and capacity for worldwide aggression, settled for little more than that. This decision, if ever explicitly made, no doubt resulted

Table 4-1. Joint Chiefs of Staff Estimate of Minimum-Risk Forces[a]

Forces	Active-duty	Reserve
Army divisions	25	8
Marine expeditionary forces[b]	4	1
Air Force fighter-attack wings	38	19
Aircraft carrier battle groups	22	. . .
Intercontinental airlift aircraft	632	. . .
Intratheater airlift aircraft	458	302
Strategic bombers	483	. . .
Intercontinental ballistic missiles	1,254	. . .
Fleet ballistic missile submarines	44	. . .

Source: William W. Kaufmann, *The 1986 Defense Budget* (Brookings, 1985), p. 3.
a. As estimated in 1982. Projected date of deployment was 1991.
b. A Marine expeditionary force is usually defined as a division and an air wing.

in part from the bill presented by the Joint Chiefs of Staff for what they considered the "requirements" of a "worldwide" war, which to them meant a conflict waged in multiple theaters, or a 3½-war strategy (table 4-1).

Fortunately, none of these strategies was ever fully tested. Assuming that Soviet leaders regularly and seriously considered launching a surprise nuclear attack on the United States—a thought that might damage the image of the unitary, rational actor—strategic deterrence apparently worked. On the other hand, while Ho Chi Minh may have ignored the forward presence of the Navy's carrier battle groups and continued his fight against South Vietnam, no one else in Moscow or Pyongyang decided to embark on a concurrent adventure. Deterrence may have worked to some extent here too.

It is too early for the base force to have undergone its reality check. What is possible, however, is to subject it to some of the standard tests that arise in the process of force planning. Such an effort may reveal something about the cost and effectiveness of the base force and how, by those measures, it compares with other and more modest proposals.

Notes

1. William W. Kaufmann, *Planning Conventional Forces, 1950–80* (Brookings, 1982), pp. 5–7.
2. *Department of Defense Annual Report, Fiscal Year 1969*, pp. 41–69, 76.
3. Ibid., pp. 77–85.

CHAPTER FIVE

THE NUCLEAR COMPONENT

EYEBROWS ARE OFTEN raised at the thought of studying thermonuclear war. But hypothetical nuclear exchanges remain an essential tool in the search for deterrence and stability. The analysis of an enemy surprise attack and U.S. retaliation can have a great deal to say about the vulnerabilities of U.S. forces, their effectiveness against a range of targets, the consequences to both sides of such an exchange, and the power as well as the credibility of the U.S. deterrent. Even a hypothetical U.S. surprise attack can tell much about an enemy's deterrent. To the extent that stability is primarily the function of survivable forces on both sides, such an analysis can also say something about pressures to accelerate the arms competition or about potential trigger-happiness in a crisis—the main sources of instability. Both types of analysis should also be an essential precondition to any deployment of an antiballistic missile (ABM) system.

New Nuclear Force Goals

Defense of the base force has not included much serious discussion of these matters. Neither the Pentagon nor the White House has revealed anything about the analyses that have led to successive reductions in U.S. strategic nuclear forces and have now culminated in the Bush-Yeltsin accord of June 17, 1992. To say this, however, is not to disparage the reductions or the agreement. Both leaders appear to anticipate not only an end to the belief that nuclear weapons can confer a meaningful military advantage on either side but also an end to nuclear competition. From the standpoint of the United States, the agreement also appears to undercut the recommendations of an

31

advisory panel to General George Lee Butler, the director of the Joint Strategic Target Planning Staff (JSTPS), which provides the specific targets and aiming points for all U.S. strategic offensive forces. The panel, according to published reports, had proposed to replace the SIOP (single integrated operational plan) with a new document that would include five separate plans. These plans would target "every reasonable adversary"—and perhaps the unreasonable ones as well—with nuclear or non-nuclear warheads. Such an approach reportedly would have required a strategic arsenal of approximately 5,000 nuclear weapons, which was close to the administration's goal of 4,700 warheads prior to the Bush-Yeltsin accord. Either total would supposedly have maintained a comfortable numerical advantage over an unlikely combination of British, French, and Chinese nuclear forces, which were estimated to expand from 1,500 to 2,000 weapons within a few years.[1] Despite this apparent concern, the United States, it is worth noting, continues to assist the British nuclear program.

Issues of Evaluation

Whether an analysis of targets preceded the new Bush-Yeltsin goal of 3,500 weapons is unclear. It will be recalled that the draft DPG had U.S. nuclear warheads directed against vital aspects of the former Soviet military establishment and emphasized that the strategic nuclear forces "must continue to hold at risk those assets and capabilities that current—and future—Russian leaders or other nuclear adversaries value most."[2] But that guidance, carefully crafted in nonquantitative language, is an open invitation to a long list of targets. Should the guidance be left to stand? Should a more seriously constrained set of targets be put in its place? And is 3,500 the right number of warheads?

Little if any light has been shed on these matters. Reasonable guesses nonetheless are possible about the nature of future nuclear arsenals in the hands of Russia, China, and other existing or potential nuclear powers. Equally feasible is an approximation of targets and aiming points—depending on the number of countries to be covered—and an estimate of the U.S. forces needed to have a significant probability of destroying the targets.

But what countries are to be covered, and under what conditions? It becomes increasingly difficult in the wake of the Bush-Yeltsin accord to imagine the United States and Russia as serious future adversaries and intense competitors. It takes a still greater leap of the imagination to suppose that the Russians—deprived by the accord of their most powerful and accurate offensive weapons—will seriously consider either a surprise nuclear attack on the United States or a nuclear strike against alerted U.S. offensive forces as the outgrowth of a non-nuclear conflict. Other nuclear adversaries with anything comparable to Russian offensive capabilities are unlikely to develop in the next ten years. In other words, a nuclear first strike, designed to take out a major portion of the U.S. offense (the submarine-based component at sea cannot currently be targeted), no longer seems to be a plausible contingency for force planning purposes. Leaving aside for the moment the issue of small-scale sneak attacks on the United States, by far the greater likelihood is that of an attack by a nuclear country on a third party. This prospect is particularly troublesome because nuclear countries of the future will probably deploy small capabilities that are highly vulnerable to preemptive attack and designed to deter equally vulnerable regional foes. Preemptive attacks become plausible in these circumstances.

This image of the future raises a host of difficult issues for U.S. policymakers, which cannot all be resolved by the most vigorous (and most desirable) measures against proliferation. For force planning purposes, however, one quite conservative option would be to maintain the capability not to target every conceivable adversary, but to cover critical military assets in two of the existing nuclear powers. The obvious candidates for such coverage are Russia and China, not necessarily because they might prove threatening to their neighbors or the United States but because from the standpoint of force size and composition they represent the largest collection of targets.

This approach may not be conservative enough to a profession that, because of the stakes, is notoriously conservative. But there is a very low probability that the United States would have to contend simultaneously with both Russia and China as well as another nuclear attacker with a significant number of special targets. The probability is still lower that, even if this implausible scenario were to unfold, the United States would lack the resources to deal with it. To begin with, not all the targets would require nuclear coverage; in some instances precision-guided munitions could also do the job. Beyond that, even if the Trident ballistic missile submarines were to maintain their

Table 5-1. Targets for U.S. Strategic Nuclear Forces, Year 2000

Target	Russia	China	Total
Nuclear			
ICBM bases	56[a]	8	64
Submarine ports	4	2	6
Bomber bases	150	. . .	150
IRBM sites	. . .	60	60
MRBM sites	. . .	50	50
Early warning and C³	50	30	80
Non-nuclear			
Ground forces	50	60	110
Tactical air forces	60	40	100
Naval forces	20	10	30
Nonurban economic			
Energy	136	28	164
Transportation	204	42	246
Total	730	330	1,060

Sources: Michael M. May, George F. Bing, and John D. Steinbruner, *Strategic Arms Reductions* (Brookings, 1988), p. 32; William W. Kaufmann, *Glasnost, Perestroika, and U.S. Defense Spending* (Brookings, 1990), table 8; and author's estimates.

a. Home bases for Russian land-mobile ICBMs.

traditional patrols (a policy that deserves reconsideration), boats in transit and in overhaul would provide a significant reserve.

Targets, Perceptions, and Forces

Exactly how many targets should be included in a new set of plans with multiple attack options is bound to be an issue. It would be difficult, however, to find more than 730 special military targets in Russia once the Bush-Yeltsin agreement is implemented, and perhaps another 330 in China, for a total of 1,060 mostly soft targets (table 5-1). For all practical purposes the planned Trident submarine force of 18 submarines, 432 launchers (some of which would consist of the D-5 ballistic missile, a hard-target killer), and no more than 1,752 warheads could by itself—under conservative assumptions—have an overall damage expectancy of nearly 86 percent against the entire target list (table 5-2). Under somewhat less conservative assumptions, the damage expectancy could rise to nearly 88 percent. Either result would exceed the arbitrary standard of 80 percent set by the Air Force many years ago.

Table 5-2. **Estimated Performance of the Trident Force**
Numbers unless otherwise specified

Item	Day-to-day operations	Crisis operations
Trident submarines	18	18
Launchers	432	432
Warheads	1,752	1,752
On-station rate (percent)	70	80
Warheads on station	1,226	1,402
Warhead availability (percent)	90	90
Warheads ready to fire	1,104	1,261
Reliability of launchers and warheads (percent)	85	85
Deliverable warheads	938	1,072
Targets	1,060	1,060
Damage expectancy (percent)	85.6	87.5

Source: Author's estimates; *Department of Defense Annual Report, Fiscal Year 1993*, p. 60; and Thomas L. Friedman, "Reducing the Russian Arms Threat," *New York Times*, June 17, 1992, p. A11.

If the Trident force alone could cover a substantial list of targets, two questions arise. First, why does the United States need as many as 3,500 warheads? And second, why is it necessary to keep ICBMs and long-range bombers for this purpose? The principal answers to the first question might be that the target list needs to be much longer and that in order to avoid a perception of U.S. weakness, the strategic forces must outnumber those of Russia or some combination of other nuclear countries.

Lengthening the target list may deserve consideration, although the cost of maintaining 500 ICBMs and a fleet of heavy bombers to deliver another 1,752 warheads would not be trivial, and the gain in effectiveness—especially if cities are taken off the target list—would be small (table 5-3). The alleged need to cater to perceptions of strength or weakness revives the hoary argument that numerical differences of no military importance would influence the behavior of potential enemies. It is an argument that sounds consequential at first glance but is pernicious on at least two counts. For years, the psychoanalysts of force planning have talked about perceptions without knowing who the key perceivers were or what they perceived. At the same time, conjectures about perceptions are an open invitation for the unscrupulous to seek additional forces without any reference to their costs and effectiveness against military targets.

Table 5-3. Incremental Cost and Effectiveness of Adding Warheads to the Trident Force on the Basis of 1,060 Targets

Item	Trident	Minuteman	B-52	B-2	B-1B	Total increment
Total warheads	1,752	500	270	172	810	1,752
Annual cost (billions of 1993 dollars)	14.4[a]	2.6	1.9[b]	4.4[b]	7.6[b]	16.5
Targetable warheads	1,261	450	216	138	648	1,452
Single-shot kill probability	.85	.85	.85	.85	.85	.85
Targets destroyed	927	984	1,012	1,029	1,048	121
Percent damage expectancy	87.5	92.8	95.5	97.1	98.9	11.4
Percent increase in cost	. . .	18.1	11.2	23.3	32.6	114.6
Percent increase in effectiveness	. . .	6.2	2.9	1.7	1.9	13.1

Source: Author's estimates.
a. Includes cost of air defense, early warning, and command-control as well as of the Trident force.
b. Includes tanker as well as bomber costs, with two tankers for each bomber.

The Triad

For twenty-five years or more the answer to the second question has been that the United States must maintain a triad of offensive nuclear forces consisting of ICBMs, SLBMs, and bombers. And this response is usually accepted without further discussion. Before accepting the triad on faith, however, it is important both to recognize the conditions under which the doctrine emerged and to remember that it does not have the force of law.

By the mid-1960s, the Air Force was trying to replace its large B-52 fleet with more advanced bombers while it continued to deploy and modernize its Minuteman ICBMs. The Navy, meanwhile, was also deploying and modernizing a force of forty-one Polaris submarines with ballistic missile launchers. The issue that arose somewhat belatedly was whether the United States really needed ICBMs and SLBMs as well as bombers—a triad that for various reasons, including interservice rivalries, already existed.

The answer that justified the triad came in several parts. All three legs of the triad had problems. The bombers were considered highly reliable and could be flown every day without blowing up, but they were potentially vulnerable to Soviet air defenses. The ICBMs and SLBMs were not very reliable and were expensive to test, but they could beat all current defenses. Therefore, the triad was worth preserving as a way to spread the risks. There was also the argument that the triad complicated the task of Soviet defenses because the bombers, the ICBMs, and the SLBMs would approach the Soviet Union at differing angles, trajectories, and speeds. Finally, the target list in the Soviet Union was growing longer and Soviet ICBMs were finally being protected in hardened silos. It was therefore necessary to retain the ICBMs for the purpose of quickly killing hard targets, while the SLBMs would attack other time-urgent targets, and the much slower bombers would mop up after the ballistic missiles and take care of the less time-sensitive targets.

A great deal has changed since these arguments justified the *fait accompli* instituted by the Air Force and Navy. Ballistic missiles are now regarded as reliable launchers, although the Air Force still cannot test its ICBMs from their operational silos. The view that risks need to be spread among three different delivery systems no longer has the force that it did thirty years ago. And hedging against failure by programming a bomber, an ICBM, and an SLBM warhead on each high-priority target is almost certainly an exercise in ultraconservatism if not an invitation to force megalomania.

Of the three legs of the triad, two of them—the ICBMs and the bombers—are the most vulnerable to attack, although this may not be a problem for the foreseeable future. Trident submarines, on the other hand, are essentially invulnerable when they are at sea, and they now have the capability to attack the entire range of fixed targets, including such hard targets as ICBM silos and deep underground bunkers. They cannot attack land-mobile targets, but neither can ICBMs or bombers. Communications with submarines are said to be difficult, but the problem has been exaggerated. In sum, the heavy operating costs of the bombers and the planned downloading of the remaining ICBMs to one warhead apiece make the Trident submarines the most efficient force of the future. In fact there is no serious reason why they should not be the only force.

To propose an arsenal of 1,752 nuclear warheads based on Trident submarines is not to suggest that the United States should move unilaterally to such an objective. There is, on the contrary, much to be said for negotiating further warhead reductions with Russia and for both powers to persuade Britain, China, and France that they can safely reduce their small, vulnerable, and costly capabilities as well.

The ABM Issue

Measures of this sort, along with tighter export controls, may help in the war against the further proliferation of atomic, biological, and chemical (ABC) weapons. But several countries have already evaded the lax controls now in place, and tighter restrictions may not prevent others from developing at least nominal ABC capabilities. Indeed, if President Bush and Secretary Cheney are correct, the number is almost certain to increase by the year 2000.

This dismal prospect has led once again to support for some form of antiballistic missile defense, a congressional mandate for the Defense Department to begin the deployment of a limited ABM system as early as possible, and requests to increase funding for the strategic defense initiative (SDI), popularly known as Star Wars. Much less publicized, but perhaps more interesting, Congress has also appropriated nearly $1 billion for improved theater-based ABM systems intended as improvements of or successors to the Patriot missile.

The United States has already had one encounter with antiballistic missile defenses. In the late 1960s and early 1970s the Defense Department designed and even began to deploy a system originally intended to defend about fifty cities, then to intercept Chinese ICBMs, and finally to protect Minuteman silos. Before another such enterprise begins, certain questions deserve public consideration.

Not the least of these questions concerns the specific nature of the threats and when they are likely to materialize. Obviously any one of the existing producers of long-range capabilities could equip another country with ICBMs, nuclear weapons, or other unconventional warheads in a rather brief period of time. So far, however, there is no public evidence that this kind of proliferation is going on, although one Russian agency is apparently committed to providing India with the components of a long-range ballistic missile. Interestingly, China, by its own efforts, seems to have deployed only eight ICBMs and one ballistic missile submarine, which suggests how costly a small capability of this sort can be.[3] Perhaps to help pay for it, the Chinese have sold shorter-range missiles to customers in the Middle East and Southwest

Asia. Estimates from the Central Intelligence Agency (CIA) suggest, however, that even countries with ballistic missiles or programs to develop them are at least a decade away from deploying anything that approximates an ICBM.[4] Nothing has been said about the accuracy or reliability of such a missile.

Because of the experience with Iraq and the suspicions about North Korea, most of the current speculation focuses on the possibility of such countries acquiring and using ABC weapons. But there is also concern about a terrorist group seizing a nuclear weapon, an insubordinate crew taking control of an armed ICBM and firing it, or a mistake of some kind resulting in the accidental launch of a missile.

Exactly which targets would be threatened by these kinds of developments is unclear. But reasons of status, lack of trust in an ally, fear of a potential enemy, or some combination of these motives have dictated the acquisition of weapons of mass destruction by most countries thus far. In the cases of Israel, China, India, and Pakistan, deterrence of a long-standing foe has usually accounted for proliferation. Nonetheless, it is impossible to rule out untoward events. Accidental launches could occur, although there is much the major nuclear powers can still do to prevent them. Other countries, by nuclear threats, might seek to deter U.S. involvement in a regional conflict. Terrorists, even without ICBMs, might try to blackmail the United States into granting their demands. Such possibilities are sufficient to demand serious consideration of defensive measures. But what kinds of defenses are relevant, how effective are they likely to be, and what might they cost?

The case for theater-based defenses is strong. It should be evident, however, that the United States will continue to have people and assets overseas that hostile elements could seize or attack without regard to air or missile defenses. And the same is likely to be true of people and assets in the United States itself.

ICBMs or SLBMs, moreover, are more difficult to intercept than Scuds or Silkworms. If the Missile Defense Act of 1991 is implemented, it will involve the construction of a single ABM site that will be limited to 100 interceptors so as to comply with the ABM treaty of 1972 (and the 1974 protocol). Such a defense would cover most, but not all, of the continental United States, depending on the range and speed of the interceptors. This probably means that Alaska, Hawaii, and Puerto Rico would fall outside its perimeter as well. It would supposedly have the capability to intercept as many as twenty or thirty reentry vehicles

Table 5-4. ABM Performance, Single Site with 100 Interceptors

Single-shot kill probability	Twenty-warhead attack			Five-warhead attack		
	Five-shot kill probability	Expected kills	Expected penetrators	Twenty-shot kill probability	Expected kills	Expected penetrators
.9	.9999	20	. . .	.9999	5	0
.8	.9997	19.9936	.0064	.9999	5	. . .
.7	.9976	19.9514	.0486	.9999	5	. . .
.6	.9898	19.7952	.2048	.9999	5	. . .
.5	.9688	19.375	.625	.9999	5	. . .
.45	.9497	18.9934	1.0066	.9999	5	. . .
.4	.9222	18.448	1.5552	.9999	5	. . .
.3	.8319	16.6386	3.3614	.9992	4.996	.004
.2	.6723	13.4464	6.5536	.9885	4.9424	.0576
.1	.4095	8.1902	11.8098	.8784	4.3921	.6079
.08	.3409	6.8184	13.1816	.8113	4.0565	.9435
.07	.3043	6.0862	13.9138	.7658	3.8288	1.1712

Source: Author's estimates.

launched by ICBMs or long-range SLBMs.[5] The Congressional Budget Office has estimated that a single site, located at Grand Forks, North Dakota, would cost $37 billion on top of the $29 billion already spent on the strategic defense initiative. The Pentagon, however, regards Grand Forks as the first step in a more ambitious deployment. Under its plan, as many as seven sites would be constructed. By 2005, the total cost of SDI would amount to at least $85 billion.[6] Annual operating and support costs for a deployment could run into the billions as well. This expanded system would require modification or abrogation of the ABM treaty.

ABM Performance

So much for costs. What about effectiveness? No data are available, but assume for a moment that a single site has the capacity to cope with an attack of up to twenty reentry vehicles. The measure of its effectiveness would presumably be the probability that its interceptors, singly or in multiple shots, could destroy a reentry vehicle. The desired level of effectiveness would, one supposes, be the disabling of all incoming warheads.

A simple calculation will suggest the difficulty of reaching this goal. Each interceptor would have to obtain an overall kill probability (combining reliability and accuracy) in the range of .6, and five interceptors would have to be fired at each of the twenty incoming objects to give virtual certainty of preventing one reentry vehicle from penetrating the defense. Such a single-shot probability of kill is not impossible to achieve, but it is rather high for such a difficult task, which must be completed in a very short time at very high speed. Moreover, if the probability were to fall to only .45, one reentry vehicle, on the average, could be expected to get through. More optimistically, if only five reentry vehicles were on their way, twenty interceptors could be assigned to each of the five warheads. Under these conditions the single-shot kill probability would have to decline to .0773 before one reentry vehicle could be expected to get through (table 5-4).

Small attacks thus may seem quite manageable and the early deployment of a single site quite sensible insurance. But the assistant secretary of defense for program analysis and evaluation, David S. C.

Chu, has complained that to deploy a system by 1996 or even 1997 would mean the omission of important performance tests and require concurrency in development and procurement, a process that Cheney had planned to eschew. Despite Chu's recommendation that any deployment be deferred until the year 2002 or 2003, the deputy secretary of defense, Donald J. Atwood, agreed to a postponement of only one year to 1998.[7] Consequently, if the deployment goes forward as now planned it will be marked by high risk as well as high cost. How effective it will be must remain uncertain.

Other Challenges

There is, in any event, a further fly in this ointment. An axiom of force planning is or should be that one should not depend on the cooperation of an adversary in the design of one's own defenses. If a loophole exists the opponent has the incentive and can usually find the time to exploit it. Recognition of this possibility, and of the amount of time it will take to deploy an ABM system to cover all of the United States, has led to the expectation that any such deployment would have to be accompanied by an expansion of the minimal antibomber defenses now in place. But even that may not be enough. Bombers, if they are not disguised as cargo aircraft and are not flying along commercial routes, may be easier to detect, identify, track, and intercept than ballistic missile reentry vehicles. Cruise missiles, however, are another matter. According to Cheney, "We would not . . . be able to detect or defend against future low-observable cruise missiles or bombers by upgrading current systems."[8] Of course, stealth vehicles may not yet have entered the proliferation pipeline; even so, the threat of long-range aircraft and existing cruise missiles is worth taking at least as seriously as the less likely threat of ballistic missiles.

There is, to be sure, a research and development program in existence known as the air defense initiative, but it has neither the interest nor the resources devoted to SDI. Meanwhile Cheney is retiring some air defense interceptors and deactivating the over-the-horizon backscatter radars designed to detect bombers before they can launch cruise missiles.[9] As for other defensive measures, no public consideration has been given to the cost and effectiveness of fallout shelters even though they would constitute a major supplement to an active defense that is unlikely to provide leakproof protection of the U.S. population. Perhaps in the circumstances SDI should stand for "selective damage insurance."

Instability

Defense loopholes are not the only problem with SDI. The Pentagon, despite its efforts to accelerate the program, has suffered from the argument that SDI undermines nuclear stability. It allegedly does so because it gives Russian leaders the impression that U.S. planners are preparing for a first strike, after which an ABM system might prove quite effective against a damaged and uncoordinated retaliation. Such a concern, admittedly, may have seemed unrealistic when the Soviet Union deployed more than 10,000 strategic nuclear warheads. But the GPALS sought by the Pentagon may look more sinister when the Russian arsenal is reduced to no more than 3,500 weapons, many of which, along with command and communications systems, could be destroyed in a preemptive strike.

To counter this impression, the Bush administration has proposed that Russia join the United States in developing a joint warning system and ABM program. But the Pentagon's eagerness to modify or scrap the ABM treaty and its reluctance to share SDI technology with its former rivals is hardly conducive to mutual trust and shared defenses, even if they prove technically feasible.

To underscore the many problems with an early deployment of ABM defenses is not to argue against the principle of GPALS, or the possibility of defenses against bombers, commercial aircraft, cruise missiles, ships with nuclear cargoes, suitcase bombs, and all the other possibilities that analysts have conjured up for so many decades. Nor is it to assert that because, once before, the United States considered both comprehensive and limited ABM defenses—and actually built a single site at Grand Forks, North Dakota, twenty years ago, only to dismantle most of it shortly thereafter—U.S. options should not be reviewed now. There is, however, a case to be made, simultaneously, for a much more determined effort, including the possible use of force, to curb the addiction to ABC proliferation and address its causes. Such an effort, admittedly, is neither glamorous nor painless. But the alternative could be an even more costly proliferation of defensive measures of all kinds and a retreat of the wealthier nations behind protective walls.

Whether the United States can afford to wait for the threats to grow more imminent remains an issue. Perhaps it cannot, even if the result is an expensive Potemkin village. But it is also worth remembering that the long-range ballistic missile threat is neither the only one nor the most urgent. The not-so-new regional strategy announced by President Bush means that U.S. forces are likely to be exposed to ABC weapons, as are U.S. allies, far sooner than the United States becomes vulnerable to rogue ICBMs. Indeed, the probability is sufficiently high, as Iraqi Scuds demonstrated, to warrant less emphasis on GPALS and a more determined effort to test and deploy an improved Patriot system that can engage reentry vehicles at longer ranges and greater altitudes with a higher probability of kill. That is where the most serious challenge lies during the next ten years.

The Case for More Cuts

The intensity of the debates over nuclear issues reflects one of the poorly acknowledged ironies of the cold war: the more the United States has struggled to improve its nuclear posture the larger its defense problems seem to have become. Indeed, despite the end of the cold war and the collapse of the Soviet Union, the Pentagon anticipates an even more dangerous world marked by the proliferation of nuclear weapons and long-range delivery systems. And while some of the concern may be attributable to self-interest, it is also symptomatic of a deeper cause, namely, that technical sophistication runs into rapidly diminishing returns against relatively simple countermeasures with big and devastating bangs.

After the expenditure of nearly $2 trillion (in 1993 dollars), the Pentagon has tacitly conceded that no one knows how to achieve a meaningful military advantage with strategic nuclear weapons and that the main, if not only, purpose of these weapons is to deter the use of nuclear weapons by others.[10] President Bush has made much the same admission with his eminently sensible decision to remove most tactical nuclear weapons from their overseas locations and from all naval ships, submarines, and aircraft. Meanwhile, General Powell wisely recognizes

Table 5-5. Numbers and Annual Cost of Alternative Nuclear Forces
Costs in billions of 1993 dollars in budget authority

Force	START treaty		Bush-Yeltsin	
	Number	Cost	Number	Cost
Minuteman III ICBMs	500	2.6	500	2.6
MX ICBM	50	2.0	. . .	. . .
Trident/C-4 missile	192	4.1	192	4.1
Trident/D-5 missile	240	6.5	240	6.5
B-52 bomber	95	3.8	30	1.2
B-1B bomber	97	6.0	90	5.6
B-2 bomber	20	4.0	20	4.0
KC-135 tanker	424	4.7	280	3.1
Air defense	. . .	0.3	. . .	0.3
Early warning, command-control	. . .	3.8	. . .	3.8
Strategic defense initiative	. . .	4.8	. . .	4.8
Total strategic	. . .	42.6	. . .	36.0

Sources: *Department of Defense Annual Report, Fiscal Year 1993*, p. 60; John G. Roos, "End of KC-135 Reengining Blow to Offshore Buys," *Armed Forces Journal International*, vol. 129 (March 1992), p. 18; and author's estimates.

that the comparative military advantage of the United States lies in its non-nuclear capabilities and technologies.

The extent to which this realism about the future role of nuclear weapons will be reflected in future editions of the base force and its costs has not yet been indicated. Implementation of the Bush-Yeltsin accord should bring down the annual real cost of the strategic nuclear offense by at least $6.6 billion, and this saving could easily be made in fewer than ten years (table 5-5). However, insistence by the Pentagon and Congress on an early deployment of GPALS is likely to offset this saving. President Bush's retirement of most tactical nuclear weapons should also permit real savings of several billion dollars during the next five years.

While most of this is all to the good, more can be done without any risk to national security. There is no longer any serious reason why the strategic nuclear arsenal cannot be reduced to a force of eighteen Trident submarines and 1,752 warheads. And there is not even the shadow of a case for continuing the deployment of nuclear bombs in Europe, when the weapons themselves have been unusable for decades and there is no enemy, in any event, against which to use them. The time has come to dismantle this anachronistic capability in its entirety.

Table 5-6. Cost of Nuclear Options
Billions of 1993 dollars in budget authority

Item	START force	Bush-Yeltsin force	Reduced force
Minuteman III	2.6	2.6	. . .
MX	2.0	. . .	. . .
Trident/C-4	4.1	4.1	5.1
Trident/D-5	6.5	6.5	5.2
B-52	3.8	1.2	. . .
B-1B	6.0	5.6	. . .
B-2	4.0	4.0	. . .
KC-135	4.7	3.1	3.1[a]
Air defense	0.3	0.3	0.3
Early warning, command and control	3.8	3.8	3.8
Strategic and tactical defense initiatives	4.8	4.8	3.0[b]
Subtotal	42.6	36.0	20.5
Artillery shells	0.9	. . .	. . .
Bombs	0.8	0.4	. . .
Cruise missiles	0.5	. . .	. . .
Subtotal	2.2	0.4	. . .
Total	44.8	36.4	20.5

Source: *Department of Defense Annual Report, Fiscal Year 1993*, p. 60; and author's estimates.
a. The 280 tankers included here would be used by the non-nuclear forces.
b. Of the total, $2 billion would be for continued ABM defense development and testing and $1 billion would go to an improved tactical defense system.

If these two steps are taken, and if a decision to deploy GPALS is deferred to the next century, the cost of the nuclear component of the base force would amount to $20.5 billion (in 1993 dollars) compared with the $42.6 billion that now appears to be allocated to this capability (table 5-6). In this respect at least, the base force can go on a stricter diet than either President Bush or Secretary Cheney has proposed.

Notes

1. R. Jeffrey Smith, "U.S. Urged to Cut 50% of A-Arms," *Washington Post*, January 6, 1992, pp. 1, 14.

2. Patrick E. Tyler, "U.S. Strategy Plan Calls for Insuring No Rivals Develop," *New York Times*, March 8, 1992, p. 14.

3. International Institute for Strategic Studies, *The Military Balance 1991–1992* (London: Brassey's for the IISS, 1991), p. 150.

4. R. Jeffrey Smith, "U.S. Moves Away From ABM Treaty," *Washington Post*, January 26, 1992, pp. A1, A22; and R. Jeffrey Smith, "'Star Wars' Lives On— Expensively," *Washington Post*, May 20, 1992, pp. A1, A18.

5. *Department of Defense Annual Report, Fiscal Year 1993*, p. 66.

6. David Mosher and Raymond Hall, "Costs of Alternative Approaches to SDI," CBO Papers, Congressional Budget Office, Washington, May 1992. This CBO study is outlined in "Congress Report Says Antimissile Defense Would Cost $37B," *Boston Globe*, May 28, 1992, pp. A4, A17.

7. R. Jeffrey Smith, "SDI Adopts 'High Risk' Procurement," *Washington Post*, July 3, 1992, p. A6; and William J. Broad, "Pentagon Plans One-Year Delay of 'Star Wars,'" *New York Times*, June 6, 1992, pp. 1, 9.

8. *Department of Defense Annual Report, Fiscal Year 1992*, p. 57.

9. *Department of Defense Annual Report, Fiscal Year 1993*, pp. 66–67.

10. Office of the Comptroller, Department of Defense, *National Defense Budget Estimates for FY 1993* (DOD, March 1992), p. 61.

CHAPTER SIX

THE NON-NUCLEAR COMPONENT

NUCLEAR FORCES have become increasingly the vermiform appendage of the base force. Its real body consists of the non-nuclear ground, tactical air, naval, and mobility forces. Whether they too can be considered overweight depends to a considerable extent on what is made of the data provided to the *New York Times* (and shortly thereafter to the *Washington Post*) in February 1992. Reportedly, the data were contained in documents that laid out certain contingencies, along with scenarios of hypothetical attacks, warning times, the magnitude of the U.S. response, and the length of the hypothetical wars that ensued. Planners from the Joint Staff apparently did the analyses of five separate contingencies and also tried to consider the implications of a resurgent-emergent global threat (REGT). Their task, presumably, was to test the adequacy of the base force in the face of these threats.[1]

Force Planning Contingencies

The most alarming of the three major contingencies has an authoritarian Russian regime, abetted by Belarus, attacking portions of Poland in order to overrun Lithuania. This contingency has supposedly been discarded because of publicity and poor taste. In another disturbing case, a revived Iraq invades Kuwait and Saudi Arabia. In the most traditional of the three contingencies, North Korea attacks South Korea under the cover of a peace initiative. Iraq and North Korea also provide the basis for the two approximately simultaneous attacks that supposedly generated the original requirement for the base force.[2]

On a much smaller scale, coups erupt in Panama and the Philippines. Although both make demands on U.S. capabilities, neither appears to require additions to the base force. Nor does the REGT, in which an authoritarian government, in what must be Russia, begins to emerge in 1994. By the year 2001 this restored tyranny has managed such a large military resurrection that it has the capability to renew the cold war and possibly begin a hot global war of unspecified dimensions. Confronted by this resurgent-emergent threat, the Defense Department undertakes a major military buildup of its own. It is not clear when this response starts, but it includes expanded forces through recruitment and possibly even the draft, as well as greatly increased military procurement in general and major weapons modernization in particular. The main message of REGT appears to be that the United States must have a plan for national mobilization, retain a selective service system, and maintain a substantial military-industrial base.[3]

Whether the three main contingencies are plausible candidates for force planning and whether the two-war concept is too conservative in light of history and the end of the cold war depends on a number of factors. One is the current and future pattern of conduct followed by the United States and its allies. The record thus far is mixed. While Desert Storm will cast a long shadow of deterrence for some time to come, it may be attenuated by subsequent problems with Iraq, Cambodia, and Yugoslavia. But only a few years have passed since the collapse of the Soviet empire; it is still too early to draw conclusions about the fate of collective or cooperative security.

It was a bold man who first ate an oyster, according to Jonathan Swift, and it would take an even bolder one to predict a new era free of violent outbursts. Similarly, it would be difficult to say that the DPG contingencies break any physical laws or that they necessarily exaggerate the dangers the United States may confront in the new era. In the circumstances, rather than argue about an uncertain future, it seems preferable, at least initially, to accept the DPG's assumptions and consider how the planners of the Joint Staff have responded to them.

Russia and Lithuania

In many ways the Russian attack on Lithuania is the most challenging assumption. According to General Powell, "The Red Army is gone."

He has also asserted that "the likelihood of a global war, and especially a major war in Europe, has disappeared before our eyes."[4] He could have added that Russia currently plans to maintain a total military establishment of no more than 1.5 million military personnel, which is slightly smaller than the base force. Nonetheless, the force planners assume that a force of twenty-four divisions—eighteen Russian and six Belarussian—seizes portions of Poland and Lithuania before NATO is able to react. The eventual NATO reply consists of what is described as an "adequate" force of twenty-four divisions and seventy fighter-attack squadrons. The United States makes a substantial contribution to the force, including 7⅓ active Army divisions, a Marine expeditionary force, forty-five Air Force fighter squadrons, four heavy bomber squadrons, and six carrier battle groups. After eighty-nine days of combat, including twenty-one days of a "very high intensity" counterattack by the United States and its allies, the aggressors are defeated.[5]

An "overwhelming" NATO force would apparently consist of the same allied contributions as before, but would include a much larger contingent of U.S. capabilities. They would consist of 11⅔ active Army divisions, two MEFs, sixty-three Air Force fighter squadrons, four heavy bomber squadrons, and eight carrier battle groups. Interestingly enough, this second scenario requires the bulk of the active-duty base force, and the combination of coups in Panama and the Philippines justifies the rest.[6]

Iraq, Kuwait, and Saudi Arabia

The hypothetical Iraqi attack, occurring sometime after 1995, manages to seize all of Kuwait as well as the major ports and airfields of northeastern Saudi Arabia. A total of twenty-one divisions accomplishes this task, about half the size of the Iraqi force estimated to have been deployed in the Kuwaiti theater of operations in 1990. Despite the increased difficulty of gaining access to Saudi Arabia, the United States manages to lead a coalition into battle with a force of 4⅔ heavy Army divisions, one MEF, fifteen Air Force fighter-attack squadrons, four heavy bomber squadrons, and three carrier battle groups. The war this time takes somewhat longer than Desert Storm. The allied coalition wins after fifty-four days of combat, seven of which involve another very high intensity, but victorious, counterattack. Coincidentally, the U.S. contribution to the NATO force considered "adequate" to defeat Russia and Belarus, combined with the U.S. units committed to the war with Iraq, adds up to most of the base force.[7]

North Korea and South Korea

Finally, there is the case of North Korean aggression against South Korea. The North, seeking initially to capture Seoul, launches a surprise attack against heavily fortified South Korean lines. The United States immediately rushes reinforcements into the theater. They consist of 5⅓ active Army divisions, two MEFs, sixteen Air Force fighter-attack squadrons, four heavy bomber squadrons, and five carrier battle groups. The South Korean–U.S. alliance defeats the North Koreans after ninety-one days of combat, including twenty-eight days of the now-familiar, very high intensity counterattack. The U.S. contribution, oddly enough, is comparable numerically to the expeditionary force the United States committed to Korea in 1950–51. Since then, U.S. combat power and effectiveness have probably doubled. The South Koreans, for their part, have developed a strong and growing economy as well as large, well-trained forces of their own. Conveniently, the U.S. contribution to the Korean campaign, combined with the U.S. forces "required" by the Kuwaiti contingency, adds up once again to the bulk of the base force.[8]

Two Wars

The forces required by the occurrence of two contingencies—one in the Persian Gulf followed by another on the Korean peninsula—are the same as they were for the individual contingencies. The two "requirements" are simply added together. However, because of shortages of pre-positioned matériel and airlift and sealift, the United States sends the required forces to Saudi Arabia before it deploys the large Korean package. As a consequence of the shortages and the subsequent delays in the reinforcement of South Korea, combat in both theaters is extended. The campaign against Iraq lasts sixteen more days; the defeat of North Korea requires sixty-six more days.[9]

Table 6-1. U.S. Forces Required by Planning Contingencies

Contingency	Army divisions	Marine expeditionary forces[a]	Air Force fighter squadrons/wings	Heavy bomber squadrons	Carrier battle groups
Lithuania-Poland					
Adequate force	$7\frac{1}{3}$	1	45/15	4	6[b]
Overwhelming force	$11\frac{2}{3}$	2	63/21	4	8[b]
Base force	12	3	78/26	4	12[c]
Persian Gulf	$4\frac{2}{3}$	1	15/5	4	3[b]
Korea	$5\frac{1}{3}$	2	$16/5\frac{1}{3}$	4	5[b]
Persian Gulf and Korea[d]	10	3	$31/10\frac{1}{3}$	4	8[b]
Base force	12	3	78/26	4	12[c]
Panama	$\frac{2}{3}$	$\frac{1}{3}$	$1\frac{1}{3}$	. . .	1[b]
Philippines	$\frac{2}{3}$	$\frac{1}{3}$	. . .	. . .	2[b]

Sources: Patrick E. Tyler, "7 Hypothetical Conflicts Foreseen by the Pentagon," *New York Times*, February 17, 1992, p. A8; Barton Gellman, "Pentagon War Scenario Spotlights Russia," *Washington Post*, February 20, 1992, pp. A1, A21; and *Department of Defense Annual Report, Fiscal Year 1993*, pp. 1, 75.

a. Each Marine expeditionary force consists of a division and an air wing.

b. These are the number of carriers deployed. Between 8 and 9 could be deployed out of a total of 12.

c. This is the total number of carriers available.

d. This is the simultaneous two-war contingency.

Implications

This collection of contingencies and the U.S. forces tested by them send several messages. Most important, whether the policymaker chooses the overwhelming U.S. force against Russia and Belarus, the pairing of the adequate force for that contingency and the package for Iraq, or the combination of the forces required in the Iraqi and Korean contingencies, with the Panama and Philippine coups thrown in to fill any gaps, the total U.S. input will always add up to the base force (table 6-1). In other words, the base force was right on the mark in 1990 and remained right on the mark in 1992. The force planners obviously deserve a commendation.

Of lesser note is the subliminal message that active-duty forces are best suited to fight the wars of the future. Only in the case of the overwhelming force against Russia and Belarus do what appear to be eighteen Air National Guard squadrons get into the fight. No doubt combat support and combat service support units would be drawn from the reserves, as they were in preparation for Desert Storm. But combat units from the reserves would presumably be useful only for rotation in the unlikely event of a more drawn out Desert Shield or in preparation for the REGT.

It is also worth reflecting that the United States has allies in all three of the main hypothetical wars: in Europe, in the Gulf, and in Korea. Yet in each instance U.S. forces play the dominant role. The message seems to be that, just as in the old days of the cold war, U.S. allies cannot be relied on to provide more than a modest, predetermined military contribution to the common effort. As in the past, force planners apparently take these contributions as unalterable and make up any deficit in requirements with U.S. capabilities.

The analyses and evaluations of the planners from the Joint Staff also raise some questions. How did they assess the combat power and effectiveness of the various forces? What roles did they assign to allied ground and tactical air forces, and to what extent did they allow one to substitute for the other? How sensitive were their results to changes in force size and composition? In other words, how much did the outcome of a particular war differ as a function of additions to or subtractions from key U.S. forces?

Desert Storm Revisited

Because these questions are likely to go unanswered by the Pentagon, it becomes necessary to look for another way to replicate the planners' results. Perhaps the most promising approach to the problem is to determine what combat power and effectiveness U.S. ground and tactical air forces would have needed relative to their opponents in order to produce the documented results of Desert Storm. The factors derived from this analysis can then be applied in the DPG's hypothetical war following Iraq's invasion of Kuwait and Saudi Arabia and compared with the results achieved by the planners of the Joint Staff. One assumption in this process is that U.S. forces would perform no less well after 1995 than they did in 1991. Another is that the campaigns can be adequately represented and compared by means of a simple model involving the direct exchange of fire between the belligerents (see the Appendix). Finally, it is assumed that the same sequence of events that occurred in Desert Storm—in particular, an air campaign followed by a U.S. and allied ground offensive—will take place in the hypothetical wars, as seems to have been the case in the analyses by the Joint Staff.

The final outcome of Desert Storm is well known. Coalition ground and air combat forces, following General Powell's insistence on the decisive use of military power, were well on their way to destroying all Iraqi resistance in the theater when the defeated Iraqi commanders were granted an armistice. Iraqi ground forces in the theater at the outset of Desert Storm allegedly consisted of forty-two divisions and 547,000 men, although it has since been estimated that most of the deployed divisions were understrength and that no more than 361,000 men were actually present. Their main combat equipment, the basis for their combat power, is said to have consisted of no more than 4,550 tanks, 2,880 armored personnel carriers, and 3,257 artillery pieces. The Iraqi air force was estimated to have approximately 500 fighter aircraft.[10]

Total coalition forces consisted of more than 700,000 men and women. The United States contributed more than 500,000 to this total, of which at least 180,000 were reservists. The United States deployed the equivalent of eight Army and two Marine Corps divisions; allied ground forces amounted to the equivalent of another seven divisions. Most of these formations were larger and better equipped than their Iraqi counterparts.[11]

The United States also deployed the bulk of the attack helicopters, fighters, and bombers, as well as aircraft carriers and other ships in the theater. In all, these components of the U.S. force consisted of nearly 500 attack helicopters and 1,200 fighter-attack aircraft, approximately 68 B-52 bombers, 6 aircraft carriers, and 100 other ships and submarines. The B-52s flew from bases outside the theater.[12]

The Desert Storm campaign took slightly more than forty-two days. The air part of it went on for thirty-eight days. The air-ground offensive occupied the remaining one hundred hours. Fighter-attack aircraft flew more than 1,100 sorties a day. They attacked a wide range of targets including Iraqi command centers and communications, air defenses, aircraft and their shelters, ABC facilities and Scud missile launchers, the transportation system leading into the Kuwaiti theater of operations, and the entrenched Iraqi ground forces.[13]

The main objectives of the air campaign were to isolate Iraqi forces from their leadership, gain command of the air, knock out the Iraqi capacity to use ABC weapons against the coalition forces and Israel, interdict the flow of reinforcements, equipment, and supplies into the Kuwaiti theater, and destroy 50 percent or more of the enemy's deployed tanks, armored personnel carriers, and artillery. The main

Table 6-2. Estimated Effects of the Desert Storm Air Campaign

Item	Number
Days devoted to the air campaign	38[a]
Sorties	43,016
Strategic targets	723
Sorties allocated	7230
Iraqi ground-force targets (42 divisions)	10,700[b]
Sorties allocated	35,786
Probability of kill per target	.15
Iraqi ground-force targets destroyed	5,368
Percent of Iraqi ground-force targets destroyed	50
Iraqi divisions available for the ground battle	21

Sources: House Armed Services Committee, *Defense for a New Era: Lessons of the Persian Gulf War* (Government Printing Office, 1992), pp. 32–33, 84–86; "Military Briefing: Excerpts from Report by Schwarzkopf on the Fighting in the Persian Gulf," *New York Times*, January 31, 1991, p. A12; Barton Gellman, "Allied Air War Struck Broadly in Iraq," *Washington Post*, June 23, 1991, pp. A1, A16; and author's estimates.

a. The campaign actually ran for more than 42 days.

b. Based on estimates of Iraqi ground-force equipment in the Kuwaiti theater of operations.

objectives of the air-ground offensive were to liberate Kuwait and destroy the remaining Iraqi ground forces.

Published data suggest that, with as many as 43,000 sorties, combat aircraft attacked about 11,500 targets, of which approximately 10,700 comprised the main equipment of the Iraqi ground forces. If, on average, each aircraft sortie against equipment had a .15 probability of killing a target, this would have meant that, among other results, the cumulative air attacks would have effectively destroyed the combat power of half the forty-two Iraqi divisions in the theater (table 6-2). This estimate, in fact, accords with the calculation of a study by the House Armed Services Committee that of the 361,000 Iraqi troops deployed, only 182,000 were left to fight at the beginning of the air-ground campaign.[14]

In the ensuing 4.2 days, suppose that twelve U.S. and allied divisions, each with three times the combat power and twelve times the effectiveness of an Iraqi division, encountered twenty-one of those divisions. Assuming that the daily effectiveness of the Iraqis was .01 while that of the attacking allies was .12, and that normal combat exchange relationships applied, the Iraqi forces would have lost nearly eighteen divisions and 155,000 men captured, wounded, or killed in 100 hours. The U.S. component, by contrast, would have suffered 485 casualties and 121 fatalities (table 6-3). Because the encirclement of the enemy was not completed, on the order of three Iraqi divisions or their equivalents and 27,000 men would have escaped in addition to the 153,000 thought to have fled during the air campaign.

Table 6-3. Estimated Effects of the Desert Storm Ground Campaign

Item	Coalition total	United States	Iraq
Divisions	12	8	21
Combat power (divisions)	36	24	21
Daily effectiveness	.12	.12	.01
Length of counterattack (days)	4.1667	4.1667	4.1667
Outcome			
Divisions surviving	11.8	7.89	3.16
Divisions lost	0.2	0.11	17.84
Casualties[a]	728	485	154,600
Fatalities[b]	182	121	38,650

Sources: Author's estimates; House Armed Services Committee, *Defense for a New Era*, pp. 32–33; Tyler, "7 Hypothetical Conflicts Foreseen by Pentagon," p. A8; and Gellman, "Pentagon War Scenario Spotlights Russia," pp. A1, A21.

a. Include wounded, killed, and captured. The calculation of coalition casualties is divisions lost × 17,000 × .25. Iraqi casualties equal divisions lost × 8,667. See Appendix for more detailed calculations.

b. Deaths only. The calculation for all forces is number of casualties × .25.

Iraq Revisited

Let us assume that the combat power and effectiveness of U.S. and allied ground forces are correctly weighted relative to Iraqi divisions. It would not be unreasonable, therefore, to expect them to perform equally well against the Iraqi forces that attack in the DPG contingency. In this hypothetical case, the Iraqis are able to commit only twenty-one divisions to their attack. The U.S. deployment is also smaller: 5⅔ divisions (including 1 MEF) and fifteen Air Force fighter-attack squadrons.[15] No mention is made in published reports of the specific contribution of Saudi Arabian or other allied forces. Some such involvement would be essential, however, since the U.S. forces could not by themselves form a sufficiently solid front to ensure containment of the Iraqis. In addition, it seems reasonable to assume that the key allies could contribute at least 2⅓ divisions to the eventual coalition counterattack.

The DPG scenario specifies that the hypothetical campaign will take fifty-four days, of which seven are devoted to what is presumably a U.S.-led offensive designed to annihilate the Iraqi ground forces.[16] It is by no means clear, however, why the campaign as a whole or the counterattack takes so long. If the smaller tactical air forces have the same kill probabilities as they appear to have had in Desert Storm, they would be able to attack the same number of targets in Iraq itself and reduce the number of effective Iraqi divisions from twenty-one to 10½ in slightly fewer than forty-five days. If a total of eight U.S. and allied divisions then proceeded to attack these divisions, they would annihilate them in fewer than four days. A total of slightly more than forty-eight days rather than the fifty-four assumed by the DPG scenario would be required for the entire campaign.

The difference is not great overall. But in the intense ground campaign, when most of the casualties would occur, the DPG forces take almost twice as long to eliminate the Iraqi ground capabilities as the same forces would require in a replay of the Desert Storm campaign.

This is a consequential discrepancy. But there is one possible explanation for it. For when eight allied divisions of the same combat power and effectiveness fight twenty-one undamaged Iraqi divisions, it takes them just under 7.5 days to achieve a total victory, approximately the same number of days said to be needed by the Joint Staff scenario. That may seem a trivial change from 3.7 days. In this instance, however, the allies could be expected to suffer more than 1,100 casualties; in the case of the shorter battle, casualties would fall by a factor of 4 to 272 (table 6-4).

Korea and Lithuania Revisited

Similar problems arise in the Korean and Lithuanian contingencies. Because of major differences in terrain, weather, and opponents in both regions, it is logical to assume that the U.S. and allied air and ground forces would prove less powerful and effective than they were in Desert Storm. Air forces, in particular, could be expected to suffer degradations in performance over time as a result of periodic stretches of bad weather as well as terrain less conducive to the location of enemy targets. However, because of the heavy fortifications along the demilitarized zone in Korea, major concentrations of North Korean ground forces would have to take place in order to achieve breakthroughs, and lucrative targets for B-52 bombers and fighter-attack aircraft would develop.

Yet that is not what appears to happen according to published reports. As many as sixty-three days would be available for U.S. airpower to reduce the combat power of the North Korean ground forces. The twenty-eight days of very high intensity counterattack, however, seem consistent with twenty-three South Korean and 7⅓ U.S. divisions fighting forty-five essentially undamaged North Korean

Table 6-4. Estimated Effects of a Hypothetical Ground Counterattack on Iraqi Forces

Item	No prior air campaign against Iraqi ground forces			Prior air campaign against Iraqi ground forces		
	Coalition total	United States	Iraq	Coalition total	United States	Iraq
Divisions	8	5⅔	21	8	5⅔	10.5[a]
Combat power (divisions)	24	17	21	24	17	10.5
Daily effectiveness	.12	.12	.01	.12	.12	.01
Length of counterattack (days)	7	7	7	3.66	3.66	3.66
Outcome						
Divisions surviving	7.74	5.48	1.26	7.94	5.62	. . .
Divisions lost	0.26	0.18	19.74	0.06	0.0425	10.5
Casualties[b]	1,105[c]	765	171,045	272	181	91,000
Fatalities[d]	276[c]	191	42,760	68	45	22,750

Sources: Tyler, "7 Hypothetical Conflicts Foreseen by the Pentagon," p. A8; Gellman, "Pentagon War Scenario Spotlights Russia," pp. A1, A21; and author's estimates.

a. The coalition air campaign reduces Iraqi divisions from 21 to 10.5.

b. Include killed, wounded, and captured. Coalition casualties equal divisions lost × 17,000 × .25. Iraqi casualties equal divisions lost × 8.667.

c. If the coalition were to annihilate enemy forces, the time taken would amount to 7.45 days. Coalition casualties would come to 1,102 and fatalities to 276.

d. Deaths only. Fatalities for all forces equal casualties × .25.

divisions (table 6-5). Similarly, in the Lithuanian case, the NATO counterattack with 8⅓ U.S. and 15⅔ allied divisions appears to go forward and defeat the full complement of twenty-four Russian and Belarussian divisions in twenty-one days without any help from the air during the previous sixty-eight days (table 6-6).

Trade-offs

Both results evoke rich memories of the cold war analyses in which the Air Force attacked its Soviet counterparts and the ground forces slugged it out at a great disadvantage with the Red Army. Not surprisingly, as each followed its own doctrines and fought its separate battles, NATO lost the war. The concept of the air-land battle was supposed to change all that, and in real life a modification of it actually did. Desert Storm represented a serious if tacit admission that ground and air forces have a great deal in common. And the implications of that recognition are large. The old claim that air and ground operations cannot be integrated into a single analysis no longer carries weight; Desert Storm did the integration. The trouble, though, is that once the targets of air and ground operations are seen to overlap on a large scale, substituting air for ground forces becomes a distinct possibility.

Fortunately the choice does not come down to one or the other. Air forces lack the ability to occupy territory, find targets in heavily forested areas (as in Vietnam), or create barriers to contain enemy ground forces. Only the Army and the Marine Corps have those capabilities. Each type of force, in fact, has unique missions and comfortable small monopolies. But Desert Storm demonstrated that airpower can duplicate the functions of the ground forces when enemy troops can be located, identified, and tracked. It follows that, in each of the published DPG contingencies, greater application of the deployed allied airpower to enemy ground forces—especially if the Air Force were to buy more genuine ground-attack aircraft—would reduce the need for Army and Marine Corps divisions.

Implications

As one example, an air campaign that essentially replicated Desert Storm and cut the hypothetical Iraqi attack force from twenty-one to

Table 6-5. Estimated Effects of a Hypothetical Ground Attack on North Korean Forces

Item	No prior air campaign against North Korean ground forces			Prior air campaign against North Korean ground forces		
	Coalition total	United States	North Korea	Coalition total	United States	North Korea
Divisions	30⅓	7⅓	45	30⅓	7⅓	30[a]
Combat power (divisions)	37⅔	14⅔	45	37⅔	14⅔	30
Daily effectiveness	.054	.08	.02	.054	.08	.02
Length of counterattack (days)	28	28	28	16.1	16.1	16.1
Outcome						
Divisions surviving	20.8	5	0.08	26.5	6.41	...
Divisions lost	9.5	2⅓	44.92	3.8	0.92	30
Casualties[b]	40,410	9,770	449,200	16,160	3906	300,000
Fatalities[c]	10,100	2,440	112,300	4040	976	75,000

Sources: Tyler, "7 Hypothetical Conflicts Foreseen by the Pentagon," p. A8; Gellman, "Pentagon War Scenario Spotlights Russia," pp. A1, A21; and author's estimates.
a. The coalition air campaign reduces North Korean divisions from 45 to 30.
b. Include killed, wounded, and captured. Coalition casualties equal divisions lost × 17,000 × .25. North Korean casualties equal divisions lost × 10,000.
c. Deaths only. Fatalities for all forces equal casualties × .25.

Table 6-6. Estimated Effects of a Hypothetical Ground Attack on Russian and Belarussian Forces

Item	No prior air campaign against Russian-Belarussian forces			Prior air campaign against Russian-Belarussian forces		
	Coalition total	United States	Russia and Belarus	Coalition total	United States	Russia and Belarus
Divisions	24	$8\frac{1}{3}$	24	24	$8\frac{1}{3}$	16[a]
Combat power (divisions)	$32\frac{1}{3}$	$16\frac{2}{3}$	24	$32\frac{1}{3}$	$16\frac{2}{3}$	16
Daily effectiveness	.04	.04	.02	.04	.04	.02
Length of counterattack (days)	21	21	21	13	13	13
Outcome						
Divisions surviving	20.4	7.1	. . .	22.5	7.8	. . .
Divisions lost	3.6	1.24	24	1.5	0.5	16
Casualties[b]	15,180	5,270	240,000	6,450	2,240	160,000
Fatalities[c]	3,795	1,318	60,000	1,610	560	40,000

Sources: Tyler, "7 Hypothetical Conflicts Foreseen by the Pentagon," p. A8; Gellman, "Pentagon War Scenario Spotlights Russia," pp. A1, A21; and author's estimates.

a. The coalition air campaign reduces the Russian-Belarussian force from 24 to 16 divisions.

b. Include killed, wounded, and captured. Coalition casualties equal divisions lost × 17,000 × .25. Russian and Belarussian casualties equal divisions lost × 10,000.

c. Deaths only. Fatalities for all forces equal casualties × .25.

10½ divisions would permit the United States to reduce its contribution to the counterattack from 5⅔ to three divisions (two Army and one Marine Corps). This contingent, along with 2⅓ allied divisions, could destroy the remaining Iraqi forces in just 5.5 days (instead of seven) and keep U.S. casualties lower than would be the case with the larger contingent of ground forces. In the case of the hypothetical North Korean attack, an air campaign that reduced the opposing ground forces by only one-third—from forty-five to thirty understrength divisions—would still allow the United States to trim its contribution from 7⅓ to three divisions (one Army and two Marine Corps) with reductions in casualties and the length of the counteroffensive. And while the attack on Poland and Lithuania may no longer be relevant to the force planning process, it is just as instructive as the other two contingencies. Even if the large allied air forces were to succeed in reducing enemy divisions by no more than one-third, from twenty-four to sixteen, the U.S. contingent could be reduced to four divisions (all Army) without affecting the outcome (table 6-7).

The authors of the draft DPG have clearly taken a cautious view of the future. The case can indeed be made that their contingencies and their insistence on a two-war strategy are simply an excuse for keeping as many of the cold war forces as they can get away with, however pure their motives. But even acceptance of their view of the new world order, their contingencies, and their strategy does not justify more than seven Army divisions, three MEFs, and twenty-six Air Force fighter-attack wings by normal defense planning standards. By comparison with these standard assessments, indeed, the base force ground and tactical air components are overdesigned and underoptimized for the kind of world foreseen by Secretary Cheney. Or to put the matter somewhat differently, the secretary has brought an extremely conservative and costly response to his troubled world.

The Navy's Role

Although the focus of the planners seems to have been on ground and tactical air forces, it is noteworthy that the Navy in general and the carrier battle groups in particular are at least represented in all the DPG's planning contingencies. Despite their "forward presence," it is not clear how they contribute to the outcomes of the Joint Staff's hypothetical wars. As one example, published reports mention the need to bottle up the Russian navy in the Baltic Sea, but the deployment of six carrier battle groups to the scene or of five off Korea and three in the vicinity of the Persian Gulf does not seem critical to winning these wars. It is true, of course, that the base force is to contain twelve carrier battle groups as well as a large-deck training carrier, of which eight would be deployable in crises of this magnitude. But the ability to deploy eight carriers and other vessels does not by itself justify a fleet of 411 ships.[17] Opposing naval forces and the major missions of the Navy have greater relevance.

Policymakers like to say that the United States needs a navy second to none or naval superiority, whatever those evocative terms might mean. More to the point, three missions are said to shape the size and composition of the Navy. Power projection is the most salient and costly of these enterprises. It comprises the carrier battle groups and the "amphibious warfare units," which include ships that look to the layman remarkably like carriers and are indeed capable of launching helicopters and certain types of fixed-wing aircraft. These capabilities permit the Navy to project ground and air forces from ship to shore. Sea control entails the destruction of enemy surface forces, antisubmarine and antiaircraft warfare, and the armed escort of individual ships or convoys. This mission involves attack submarines, surface combatants, long-range patrol aircraft, and mines. But it could also draw on carrier battle groups to help gain command of the seas in the initial stages of a major war. Finally, forward presence, a naval favorite now adopted by the entire Defense Department, allegedly requires the continuous patrol of carrier battle groups, amphibious units, and other naval forces in such waters as the Atlantic, Pacific, and Indian oceans and the Mediterranean Sea. Like the role of policemen on the beat, their functions are to move quickly to points of crisis, deter attacks, provide the leading edge of U.S. military power in the event of crisis, and win friends and influence people through port calls and other such activities.[18]

Navy policy, it should be added, requires (at least in principle) that every unit on station must have two backups available for peacetime rotation. Thus if national policy dictates that the Navy (which often sets the policy) must keep four carrier battle groups on station in the Mediterranean and the western Pacific, that sets a "requirement" for a total of twelve carrier battle groups in the naval inventory.[19]

Table 6-7. Estimated Effects of Hypothetical Ground Attacks with Reduced U.S. Contributions (All Enemy Ground Forces Reduced by Prior Air Campaigns)

Item	Persian Gulf		Korea		Poland and Lithuania	
	Coalition total	United States	Coalition total	United States	Coalition total	United States
Divisions	$5\frac{1}{3}$	3[a]	26	3[b]	$19\frac{2}{3}$	4[c]
Combat power (divisions)	16	9	32	6	$23\frac{1}{3}$	8
Daily effectiveness	.12	.12	.054	.08	.04	.04
Length of counterattack (days)	5.5	5.5[a]	19.7	9.7[b]	18.4	18.4[c]
Outcome						
Divisions surviving	5.237	2.95	21.353	2.464	17.3	3.5
Divisions lost	.0966	0.05	4.647	0.536	2.4	0.5
Casualties[d]	410	225	19,750	2,278	10,170	2,070
Fatalities[e]	103	56	4,937	570	2,540	517

Sources: Tables 6-4, 6-5, and 6-6; and author's estimates.
a. The Joint Staff would require 5 2/3 U.S. divisions and 7 days of counterattack.
b. The Joint Staff would require 7 1/3 U.S. divisions and 28 days of counterattack.
c. The Joint Staff would require 8 1/3 U.S. divisions and 21 days of counterattack.
d. Include killed, wounded, and captured. Coalition casualties equal divisions lost × 17,000 × .25.
e. Deaths only. Fatalities equal casualties × .25.

Naval Arms Control

A process that sets requirements independent of specific, if hypothetical, enemies is the equivalent of striking gold, and the Navy has mined it with enthusiasm. But there is no escaping two facts. The first is that the Navy has chosen the most costly possible way of exercising a forward presence without being able to explain how that presence makes a difference to U.S. security. The second is that the only possible challenge to sea control—the most important of the Navy's three missions—would come from the Russian navy, which is in serious disarray. It has been evident for some time, moreover, that Moscow would be delighted to engage the United States in negotiations to reduce naval forces. Unless the Navy is now willing to repudiate its long-standing arguments about the relationship between the Russian threat and the composition of the U.S. fleet, these reductions surely make sense. It would certainly be desirable to obtain a major cut in Russian attack submarines, which are the main threat to sea control. In return, the Navy could trade in carriers—something it may have to do anyway—which Moscow has seen as a major threat to the Russian homeland. Such reductions would reduce the operating costs of both fleets and obviate the need for the Navy to build yet another nuclear-powered aircraft carrier, at a cost of more than $4 billion, and engage in an early modernization of its force of attack submarines.[20]

Power Projection

Even if resistance to naval arms reductions continues, however, much can still be done to rationalize U.S. naval forces. A first step in that direction is to recognize the limits on the utility of carrier battle groups. These units of account justify more than 50 percent of the Navy's ships and most of its aviation. They are expensive to acquire and operate. They are difficult to sink but relatively easy to disable. Because of limited deck and storage space, even on the largest modern carriers, the complement of fighter-attack aircraft is unlikely to exceed sixty, and as many as twenty of them would be dedicated to the carrier's defense (table 6-8). The implications of these constraints are twofold. Ships launching cruise missiles, as they did in Desert Storm,

Table 6-8. Composition of a Navy Air Wing
Number of aircraft

Aircraft	Conventional wing	Transitional wing	Theodore Roosevelt wing
F-14 fighter	24	20	20
F/A-18 fighter-attack	24	20	20
A-6 attack	10	16	20
KA-6	4	. . .	. . .
EA-6B	4	5	5
E-2C	4	5	5
S-3	6	6	6
SH-3/SH-60F (helicopter)	6	6	6
HH-60 (helicopter)	. . .	2	2
Total	82	80	84

Source: *Department of Defense Annual Report, Fiscal Year 1993*, p. 84, table 13.

are likely to become more efficient than carriers in projecting power ashore. And when land bases are available, the Air Force is more efficient than the Navy in attacking land-based (and even some sea-based) targets. Air Force units have also demonstrated that they can deploy with great speed to distant theaters.

This is not to suggest that the Navy should mothball all its carrier battle groups. They may not be competitive with Air Force wings in standard scenarios, but they have a monopoly on the provision of floating bases. Such an asset can prove of great value in areas where land bases do not exist, are not made available, or have been seized by an enemy. Carriers can no longer look for justification to island-hopping campaigns in the Pacific, and when used for forward presence they are expensive cops on mostly mean streets. But they are an important if expensive emergency service, capable in conjunction with amphibious forces, of establishing a beachhead on hostile shores or providing air cover in special situations.

As always, the issue is not whether to have carrier battle groups but how many of them to have. Forward presence or simply providing carriers as background scenery in DPG scenarios is hardly sufficient reason for maintaining twelve carrier battle groups. Of course they are nice to have, but only contingencies in which the carrier battle groups perform their unique functions can justify a particular number. Under present circumstances, it remains difficult to imagine a crisis—such as another confrontation with Libya or air cover in the Balkans—that would require more than four carriers on line at any one time. A fleet of six carrier battle groups would suffice to generate a fighting force of four, provided only that the carriers were based in the United States and that periodic appearances of major naval units substituted for a continuous but much smaller forward presence.

Sea Control

Although the carrier battle groups are the most expensive component of the Navy's general purpose forces, the antisubmarine warfare (ASW) capabilities come in a strong second. The published versions of the DPG contingencies do not address these capabilities, and Secretary Cheney's annual defense report provides no rationale for them. Yet the programmed number of attack submarines, patrol aircraft, sophisticated mines, and many surface combatants are very much a product of the cold war. Indeed, without the old Soviet threat, it is difficult to justify the need to place elaborate barriers in the way of enemy submarines and surface combatants or to imagine the possibility of non-nuclear wars long enough to necessitate the resupply of overseas forces with large, protected convoys of merchant and other ships.

Obliquely, it is true, the administration strategy and the DPG contingencies do make a statement about the amount of coverage to buy in this area. A conflict with Russia and Belarus could conceivably activate Russian fleets in the Atlantic and the Pacific as well as in the Baltic, but published reports of this contingency do not indicate that it would result in a major war at sea. Simultaneous wars in the Middle East and Korea, on the other hand, would require the establishment of sea lines of communication in several waters. But the DPG scenarios do not assume that Russia would side with the Iraqis or the North Koreans and threaten the sea-lanes. None of the individual wars, in any event, is particularly long. And while the combination of hypothetical attacks by Iraq and North Korea produces combat lasting 227 days, only 35 of them seem to involve intensive fighting.[21] In the circumstances, and with plans for continued pre-positioning of matériel in Europe and Korea, and maritime pre-positioning ships in other areas, the capability to conduct an elaborate ASW campaign and escort convoys in two oceans seems to be another conservative and expensive insurance policy. Even a relatively austere capability to assure sea control in one ocean is arguably an exaggerated response to a Russian

Table 6-9. An Alternative to the Base Force Navy

Active-duty ships and submarines	Base force number (1997)	Alternative number
Aircraft carriers[a]	13	7
Surface combatants	143	93
Attack submarines	79	51
Amphibious ships	49	32
Mine warfare ships	15	15
Other support ships	96	62
Total	395[b]	260[b]

Sources: *Department of Defense Annual Report, Fiscal Year 1993*, p. 75, table 11; and author's estimates.
a. All aircraft carriers, including ships in extended overhaul and the training carrier.
b. Total excludes ballistic missile submarines, their support ships, and mobilization forces.

threat that the administration finds hard to define for the next ten years (table 6-9). Other naval powers of consequence are not now on the horizon.

Strategic Mobility

Pre-positioned equipment and supplies on land, maritime pre-positioning ships of various kinds, and airlift and sealift are major components of the base force. They also permit the United States to economize on the acquisition of combat forces. It would be possible, in principle, to station enough capabilities in Europe, the Middle East, and Korea to deal with each of the DPG contingencies. But, basing problems aside, the costs would be very high, and the flexibility to deal with other contingencies would be compromised. Strategic mobility, by contrast, allows the bulk of the U.S. combat forces to be based in the United States, from which they can be deployed as the president and Congress determine. How well the system would work, however, depends on such factors as warning and the willingness of policymakers to exploit it and the mix of deployed forces, pre-positioning, airlift, and sealift.

The Pentagon's goals for the deployment of combat forces are high. To deal with contingencies in Europe, the plan is to reinforce existing units in central Europe with two Army divisions along with unspecified tactical fighter squadrons within fifteen days. At the same time, two Marine expeditionary brigades would deploy to Norway. It should be noted that these are simply scaled-down versions of the deployments that were planned when the Warsaw Pact still existed; thus the equipment and supplies pre-positioned for the arriving forces have been in place for some time.[22]

To respond to contingencies outside of Europe, the goal is to deploy approximately five Army divisions, one MEF, and unspecified tactical fighter squadrons within eight weeks. These deployments would depend heavily on airlift, pre-positioned matériel on ships, and fast sealift.[23] They would just about satisfy the DPG requirement for a force of $5\frac{2}{3}$ divisions in forty-seven days to oppose an Iraqi attack on Kuwait and Saudi Arabia, depending on how fast air and ground forces could be moved in to block further Iraqi advances. But a North Korean attack on South Korea, supposedly with little warning, would have to be contained primarily by South Korean forces until U.S. reinforcements arrived. And even then the capacity to deploy six divisions in eight weeks would fall short of the DPG requirement for seven U.S. divisions, presumably within a maximum of sixty-three days. Fortunately, in the event of the two-war case, the attacks occur sequentially so that the U.S. deployments to Saudi Arabia would occur first, followed by reinforcements to Korea. South Korean forces would have to fend pretty much for themselves during a substantial portion of these conflicts.[24]

These deployment plans, when matched with the DPG scenarios and requirements, suggest several hypotheses of relevance to the size and composition of the base force. The first of these hypotheses is that the South Koreans must be far more capable of defending themselves than the DPG scenarios assume when they set a requirement for such large U.S. reinforcements. Otherwise South Korean forces could not have held off massive North Korean attacks for perhaps as many as three months in the two-war case. The second hypothesis is that the Pentagon does not take the two-war strategy very seriously. Otherwise it would insist on a much more robust program of pre-positioning and mobility than it has proposed. The third hypothesis is that the non-nuclear component of the base force still reflects the assumptions of the cold war. Otherwise the Pentagon would not still be planning to deploy heavy Army divisions to Germany in fifteen days and send Marine brigades to Norway. A final hypothesis, in light of the others, has to be that the most expensive portion of the base force is inflated out of all proportion to the demands to which the Pentagon believes it would actually have to respond. Its leaders talk about a two-war

Table 6-10. Numbers and Annual Cost of an Alternative to the Base Force Non-Nuclear Capabilities
Costs in billions of 1993 dollars in budget authority

Item	Base force		Alternative	
	Number	Cost	Number	Cost
Ground force divisions				
Active				
Army	12	40.2	7	23.7
Marine Corps	3	5.0	3	5.0
Reserve				
Army	6	3.8	6	3.8
Marine Corps	1	0.6	1	0.6
Special operations forces	. . .	1.8	. . .	1.8
Land-based tactical air wings				
Active				
Marine Corps	3	6.8	3	6.8
Air Force	15	29.7	15	29.7
Reserve				
Marine Corps	1	0.6	1	0.6
Air Force	11	4.3	11	4.3
Naval forces				
Carrier battle groups				
(carriers/ships)	12/200	49.8	6/114	24.9
Amphibious forces (ships)	77	6.8	58	4.5
Sea control forces (ships)	118	14.8	87	13.5
Strategic mobility				
Airlift aircraft	820	11.1	820	11.1
Sealift and pre-positioning				
ships	220	2.6	220	2.6
Total annual cost	. . .	177.9	. . .	132.9

Sources: *Department of Defense Annual Report, Fiscal Year 1993*, pp. 69, 75, 81–83, 94, 139; and author's estimates.

strategy, but in the critical area of strategic mobility they have developed what amounts to a one-war plan, given the DPG requirements for ground, air, and naval forces.

Conclusions

If what the Pentagon has actually amounts to a one-war plan, the implications for the base force are considerable. Either the mobility program must be considerably expanded or the forces should be cut. The latter solution is almost certainly the only feasible one; it also appears to be the most sensible one. By all indications the base force is well out on the flat of the effectiveness curve in regard to ground and naval forces. To scale back these forces would not result in any loss of performance in the DPG contingencies. It could, however, leave the United States with a very powerful one-war capability and would make that capability much more deployable for a genuine two-war contingency (table 6-10). The issue thus is much the same as with respect to the nuclear component: not whether to put the base force on a diet, but how far and how fast to go in taking out the fat.

Notes

1. Patrick E. Tyler, "Pentagon Imagines New Enemies to Fight in Post-Cold-War Era," *New York Times*, February 17, 1992, pp. A1, A8; Patrick E. Tyler, "7 Hypothetical Conflicts Foreseen by the Pentagon," *New York Times*, February 17, 1992, p. A8; and Barton Gellman, "Pentagon War Scenario Spotlights Russia," *Washington Post*, February 20, 1992, pp. A1, A21.

2. Ibid.

3. Ibid.

4. John W. Mashek, "140,000 Cuts Sought in Reserve, Guard," *Boston Globe*, March 27, 1992, p. 12.

5. Tyler, "7 Hypothetical Conflicts Foreseen"; and Gellman, "Pentagon War Scenario Spotlights Russia."

6. Gellman, "Pentagon War Scenario Spotlights Russia," p. A21.

7. Tyler, "7 Hypothetical Conflicts Foreseen"; and Gellman, "Pentagon War Scenario Spotlights Russia."

8. Ibid.

9. Gellman, "Pentagon War Scenario Spotlights Russia," p. A21.

10. House Armed Services Committee, *Defense for a New Era: Lessons of the Persian Gulf War* (Government Printing Office, 1992), pp. 32–33; and International Institute for Strategic Studies, *The Military Balance, 1988–1989* (London, Autumn 1988), pp. 101–02. See also Eric Schmitt, "Study Lists Lower Tally of Iraqi Troops in Gulf War," *New York Times*, April 24, 1992, p. A6; and John Lancaster, "Report: Allies Faced Only 183,000 Iraqis," *Washington Post*, April 24, 1992, p. A25.

11. R. W. Apple, Jr., "Combat: Raids Said to Badly Delay Baghdad Messages to Front," *New York Times*, February 11, 1991, pp. A12, A13; Rick Atkinson and Ann Devroy, "U.S. Claims Iraqi Nuclear Reactors Hit Hard," *Washington Post*, January 21, 1991, pp. A1, A25; Michael R. Gordon, "U.S. Says Its Troops Won't Be Rotated until Crisis Is Over: Pressure on Iraq," *New York Times*, November 10, 1990, pp. 1, 8; and House Armed Services Committee, *Defense for a New Era*, map following p. xiii.

12. Department of Defense, *Conduct of the Persian Gulf War: Final Report to Congress*, appendix T: "Performance of Selected Weapons Systems" (April 1992), pp. T-3 to T-120, T-205 to T-216; and *Department of Defense Annual Report, Fiscal Year 1993*, p. 75.

13. DOD, *Conduct of the Persian Gulf War*, appendix T, pp. T-3 to T-120; Barton Gellman, "Allied Air War Struck Broadly in Iraq," *Washington Post*, June 23, 1991, pp. A1, A16; "Military Briefing: Excerpts from Report by Schwarzkopf on the Fighting in

the Persian Gulf," *New York Times*, January 31, 1991, p. A12; and House Armed Services Committee, *Defense for a New Era*, pp. 83–89.

14. House Armed Services Committee, *Defense for a New Era*, pp. 32–33.

15. Gellman, "Pentagon War Scenario Spotlights Russia"; and Tyler, "7 Hypothetical Conflicts Foreseen."

16. Ibid.

17. Gellman, "Pentagon War Scenario Spotlights Russia"; and *Department of Defense Annual Report, Fiscal Year 1993*, table 11, p. 75.

18. William W. Kaufmann, *A Thoroughly Efficient Navy* (Brookings, 1987), pp. 12–13, 73, 89–91, 117–21.

19. Ibid., pp. 121–23; and *Department of Defense Annual Report, Fiscal Year 1993*, pp. 75–77.

20. Raymond Hall, "Selected Weapons Costs from the President's 1993 Program," CBO memorandum, Congressional Budget Office, May 29, 1992, p. N-6.

21. Tyler, "7 Hypothetical Conflicts Foreseen"; and Gellman, "Pentagon War Scenario Spotlights Russia."

22. *Department of Defense Annual Report, Fiscal Year 1993*, p. 98.

23. Ibid., pp. 97–98.

24. Tyler, "7 Hypothetical Conflicts Foreseen"; and Gellman, "Pentagon War Scenario Spotlights Russia."

CHAPTER SEVEN

ISSUES AND CHOICES

SECRETARY CHENEY obviously believes in the Micawber strategy. Mr. Micawber, it will be remembered from *David Copperfield*, announced "Annual income twenty pounds, annual expenditure nineteen nineteen six, result happiness. Annual income twenty pounds, annual expenditure twenty pounds ought and six, result misery." In a similar vein, Cheney has proclaimed, "We face a fundamental choice. We can make the investment required to maintain the strategic depth we have achieved, or we can fail to secure our advantages, and watch threats grow while our capabilities weaken."[1] In other words, happiness with the base force, misery without it.

Three Options

Would that life were that simple; unfortunately it is not. Issues abound and so do choices. Not all of them can be explored and their implications translated into military forces and defense budgets. But no one is arguing seriously for a return to the budgets of the cold war. Nor is there much of a case, despite Cheney's fears, for returning to the relative isolation and the tiny defense budgets of the 1920s and 1930s. As matters now stand, a base force costing nearly $238 billion in 1993 dollars probably occupies the high end of the range of foreseeable possibilities. A much more modest force, costing approximately $135 billion, would stand at the low end of the range. A somewhat larger capability, intended to perform many but not all the functions of the base force, would have an annual budget of $173 billion (table 7-1). Other forces could also be constructed within this range of possibilities. The three forces chosen, however, should give a reason-

Table 7-1. Annual Cost of Selected Force Options
Billions of 1993 dollars in budget authority

Item	Base force	Force 2	Force 3
Strategic nuclear forces	39.3	20.5	11.2
Tactical nuclear forces	0.4	. . .	. . .
Ground forces			
Active duty			
Army	40.2	23.7	15.6
Marine Corps	5.0	5.0	5.0
Reserve			
Army	3.8	3.8	3.8
Marine Corps	0.6	0.6	0.6
Land-based tactical air forces			
Active duty			
Marine Corps	6.8	6.8	6.8
Air Force	29.7	29.7	21.8
Reserve			
Marine Corps	0.6	0.6	0.6
Air Force	4.3	4.3	4.3
Naval forces			
Carrier battle groups	49.8	24.9	20.8
Amphibious lift	6.8	4.5	2.3
Sea control	14.8	13.5	6.8
Special operations forces	1.8	1.8	1.8
Airlift and sealift			
Airlift	11.1	11.1	11.1
Sealift	2.6	2.6	2.6
National intelligence and communications	19.9	19.9	19.9
Total	237.5	173.3	135.0

Source: Author's estimates.

able approximation of the kinds of choices that deserve consideration. For purposes of simplicity, the base force keeps its name, the middle ground is labeled force 2, and the lowest option hereafter is force 3.

International Prospects

One of the most important but overlooked factors in shaping U.S. defense forces and budgets is what the planners take to be a plausible future state of the world and the kinds of demands it might make on U.S. military capabilities. A relatively benign international prospect such as some anticipated at the end of the cold war would not contain the dangers necessary to justify a major defense effort on the part of the United States; indeed it would call for very little effort at all. Thus far, however, that is not the state of the world that appears to be emerging. Nor is it the set of conditions that the base force is designed to reflect. The expectations of its designers are that, despite the end of the cold war and the conclusion of the Bush-Yeltsin agreement, nuclear deterrence of existing nuclear powers and of proliferators will remain an essential function of the armed forces. So, apparently, will the maintenance of NATO and a U.S. military presence in Europe, including a nuclear component intended to demonstrate "the United States commitment to the defense of that continent" and to "serve as the link between conventional and strategic nuclear forces."[2] In addition, many regional threats of a non-nuclear nature are foreseen, ranging from coups in such sensitive areas as Panama and the Philippines to major aggression in the Middle East and Northeast Asia. And although nothing public has been so indicated, naval forces would presumably be in demand for the projection of power by carrier battle groups and amphibious forces, protection of the sea-lanes from enemy raiders, and peacetime patrols to reassure friends and deter potential enemies.

Force 2 foresees many of the same dangers. There is more skepticism, however, about the extent of the demand for both nuclear and non-nuclear forces in general, about the desirability of using expensive military capabilities as a way of retaining a place at the European political table, and about the case for the proposed naval forces, especially if arms control measures are applied to sea-based as well as land-based capabilities. The thinking behind force 3 is somewhat different. The view here is that the United States, by vigorous action in conjunction with allies, can forestall many of the dangers about which the base force and force 2 are concerned. Such action could substitute for major nuclear and non-nuclear components of the armed forces. In sum, instead of standing by until the fires had been set, we would take measures to remove the causes and the tinder leading to the conflagrations.

The future foreseen as the context for the base force clearly makes the greatest demands on U.S. military power. The forces are commensurately large and expensive. They can also be seen as a conservative response to an uncertain future. By contrast, the contention embodied in force 3 is that the future can be controlled, forces substantially reduced, and costs brought down by more than 40 percent. The choice thus has somewhat less to do with force requirements

related to specific contingencies than with the risks of having been too
optimistic about the future and the costs of having been too conservative
in this assessment.

Hedges and Opportunity Costs

A "well-placed officer" has been quoted as saying in favor of the
conservative choice: "I have never been run over by a truck yet, but
to say it's never going to happen is pretty tough. That's why I have
life insurance, and so do you."[3] It seems likely, however, that the
officer would react differently if he had to pay an additional premium
for this part of his insurance. Assuming that he was a moderately
rational person, he would acknowledge that he has limited resources
and other important uses for them. He might well decide, under the
circumstances, that the probability of his being hit by a truck is very
low and that the added coverage is not worth the cost in light of other
more likely dangers, such as his imminent retirement, with which he
will have to cope.

It will be said yet again that gambles must not be taken with the
nation's security. Even if the risks are low the stakes are too high.
Better, therefore, to buy the hedges, whatever their cost, rather than
live with the risks. No advocate of the base force suggests, however,
that the Pentagon should hedge against the risk of madmen firing
ICBMs at the United States by buying fallout shelters. In short, large
and small risks exist everywhere, and so do opportunity costs. Is it
better to spend $5 billion on the known benefits of Head Start than on
a defense against a threat that does not seem highly probable but could
have devastating consequences if it did occur? Is GPALS, the triad,
or a hedge against major simultaneous non-nuclear attacks a better
buy than an investment in national infrastructure or deficit reduction?
The relative risks, payoffs, and net benefits to the country of these
choices may not be possible to measure in any systematic way, but
they deserve consideration and they make up much of what is at issue
between the base force and force 3.

Efficiency

By comparison, the relative efficiency of the base force in the
hypothetical pursuit of its objectives is a relatively simple matter to

measure. And for all practical purposes, efficiency is what is at issue between the base force and force 2. There are, admittedly, some problems to overcome in trying to resolve the issue. It still remains unclear whether the threats and contingencies of the DPG came before or after the birth of the base force and whether tests of efficiency are the right ones to apply to the labors of the Joint Staff planners. There are bound to be questions as well about the goals and the inputs used in attempting to measure the effectiveness of the two forces. But at the least the tests are standardized and the goals are the same for both capabilities. The inputs in all cases, moreover, are consistent with conservative assumptions about the performance of nuclear forces and with either the known outcome of Desert Storm or the hypothetical results reached by the Joint Staff. It is worth noting in this connection that General H. Norman Schwarzkopf, the commander of Desert Storm, reportedly would have liked a numerical advantage of three to one over the Iraqi forces in the Kuwaiti theater of operations. He was willing, however, to settle for less because of the edge he would acquire from air superiority, the quality of U.S. ground forces, their tactical mobility, and better intelligence.[4]

Nuclear Comparisons

What emerges from a comparison of the base force with force 2? In the case of the nuclear capabilities the base force component proposed under the Bush-Yeltsin agreement would presumably consist of a triad of ICBMs, bombers, and SLBMs with a maximum of 3,500 warheads (table 7-2). Such a force, on a generated alert, attacking a list of 1,060 targets, could be expected to achieve a damage expectancy of nearly 99 percent, or 1,047 targets destroyed (table 7-3).

Force 2 would not do so well in a numerical sense. With an offensive force consisting only of 18 Trident submarines, it would contain an arsenal of 1,752 nuclear warheads (table 7-2). Against the same list of 1,060 targets, it could be expected to achieve a damage expectancy of about 87 percent, or 927 targets destroyed. This would still be well above a damage expectancy of 80 percent usually sought by the Air Force. It would, however, fall short of the base force performance by nearly 12 percent (table 7-3). What that would signify is difficult to say, since in the eerie world of nuclear exchanges there can only be

Table 7-2. **Numbers and Annual Cost of Strategic Nuclear Forces**
Costs in billions of 1993 dollars in budget authority

Item	Base force			Force 2			Force 3		
	Launchers	Warheads	Cost	Launchers	Warheads	Cost	Launchers	Warheads	Cost
Minuteman ICBM	500	500	2.6	...	...	...	...	...	...
Trident (C-4 SLBM)	192	768	4.1	240[a]	984	5.1	240	984	5.1
Trident (D-5 SLBM)	240	984	6.5	192[a]	768	5.2	...	...	...
B-1B bomber	90	720	5.6	...	...	...	...	...	...
B-2A bomber	20	160	4.0	...	...	...	...	...	...
B-52 bomber	30	368	1.2	...	...	...	...	...	...
KC-135 tanker	280	...	3.1	280	...	3.1	...	...	...
Air defense	...	...	0.3	...	...	0.3	...	...	0.3
Intelligence and communications	...	...	3.8	...	...	3.8	...	...	3.8
Antiballistic missile defense									
Strategic defense initiative	...	...	7.0	...	...	2.0	...	...	1.0
Tactical defense initiative	...	...	1.1	...	...	1.0	...	...	1.0
Total	1,072[b]	3,500	39.3	432[b]	1,752	20.5	240	984	11.2

Sources: *Department of Defense Annual Report, Fiscal Year 1993*, pp. 60, 137; and author's estimates.
a. These SLBMs could be loaded with 3,456 warheads. In other words, were it not for the restrictions placed on SLBM loadings, force 2 could have essentially the same number of warheads as the base force at 52 percent of the cost.
b. Does not include the 280 KC-135 tankers.

Table 7-3. Performance of the Three Strategic Nuclear Forces on Generated Alert

Item	Base force	Force 2	Force 3
Total warheads	3,500	1,752	984
Available warheads			
ICBM	450	. . .	. . .
SLBM	1,261	1,261	708
Bomber	998	. . .	. . .
Total	2,709	1,261	708
Total targets (Russia and China)	1,060	1,060	1,060
Damage expectancy			
Targets destroyed	1,047	927	602
Percent destroyed	98.8	87.5	56.8
Targets in Russia only	730	730	730
Damage expectancy			
Targets destroyed	729	688	602
Percent destroyed	99.9	94.3	82.4
Targets in China only	330	330	330
Damage expectancy			
Targets destroyed	330	330	323
Percent destroyed	100	99.9	97.9

Source: Author's estimates.

relative losers. What is evident, however, is that while the base force component is more effective in blowing up targets than force 2 by 12 percent, it is also more expensive by a factor of at least two, leaving aside the costs of the strategic and tactical defense initiatives. Moreover, if additional warheads were wanted, the Trident force, at no real additional cost, could carry 3,456 warheads and achieve a damage expectancy of about 98 percent, or 1,043 targets destroyed, a performance virtually identical with that of a base force triad (table 7-3). Admittedly, the Bush-Yeltsin accord forecloses this option, but then arms control negotiators have always preferred ideology about the wickedness of MIRVs over efficiency.

Force 3 does not pretend to cover the standard list of 1,060 targets. The position, rather, is that to treat Russia as a potential enemy is anachronistic, and that Washington and Moscow should begin cooperating to reduce the nuclear warheads on each side to fewer than 1,000. At the same time they should work to minimize proliferation and deter countries that already have nuclear weapons from using them. Accordingly, only the Chinese contingency is used for force planning purposes and the Trident force is cut to 10 ballistic missile submarines, 240 C-4 launchers, and 984 warheads (table 7-2). This arsenal, on a generated alert, could attack the 330 targets in China with a damage expectancy of nearly 98 percent, or the destruction of 323 out of 330 targets. If, despite the cooperative efforts, Russia were to become an imminent threat, the same arsenal (as an alternative) could obtain a damage expectancy of slightly better than 82 percent against 730 targets. As many as 22 targets in Russia would not be attacked at all (table 7-3).

The budget for the strategic nuclear component of the base force allows sufficient funds to begin deployment of one ABM site in 1997. It also provides for a more effective theater-based defense against shorter-range ballistic missiles. Force 2 continues a vigorous research and development program on GPALS but does not fund any deployment because of the need for continued test and evaluation of the system. It also pushes ahead with a follow-on to the Patriot missile for the defense of U.S. troops in a theater. Force 3 abandons any effort to develop an operational ABM defense. It gives modest research support to the strategic defense initiative and concentrates the bulk of its research resources in this area on theater-based defenses.

There remains a major uncertainty not only about the likelihood of ICBM proliferation for some years to come but also about the number, accuracy, and reliability of the missiles that could reach the United States. Mystery surrounds the expected performance of a one-site GPALS system as well. Consequently, it is not yet possible to say much about the performance or utility of the system. However, the probability is high that its effectiveness will be low for some years to come. If only one warhead with a yield of 100 kilotons were to land in a densely populated U.S. city, it could result in prompt fatalities of 1 million or more. Total casualties would run still higher.

The original strategic component of the base force, including funds for an initial deployment of GPALS, would have cost an estimated $46 billion (in 1993 dollars). However, the Bush-Yeltsin agreement should permit annual costs to be reduced by nearly $7 billion, to $39 billion. The capabilities in force 2, with only a modest loss in effectiveness, would cost just $20.5 billion, and the strategic nuclear component of force 3 comes to a total of $11.2 billion because of its less ambitious objectives (table 7-2).

It is assumed that the base force will budget on the order of $400 million a year to maintain a modest nuclear capability in Europe, based on dual-capable aircraft stationed there. Since the logic of this costly little gesture escapes the planners of force 2 and force 3, they remove the weapons from Europe and delete the funds from their budgets. Both take the position that the threat of a tactical use of nuclear weapons by the United States in the event of a breakdown of NATO's non-nuclear defenses has been hollow for many years. To continue it after the threat has vanished is not only silly but a waste of money. As a ticket of admission to the councils of Europe it is probably useless as well. If the European allies want a continued U.S. involvement in their affairs, they will ask for it, as they have done for so many years. If they do not want it, a U.S. military presence—nuclear or non-nuclear—is unlikely to change their minds.

Whether or not the nuclear era has come to an end, non-nuclear forces continue to be the big spenders of the U.S. defense budget and have regained their prominence as the principal expression of U.S. military power. That said, the question remains: how much of that power is enough and how much is too much?

Ground and Tactical Air Forces

The base force goal for land-based tactical air and ground forces is only one possible answer to the question. Forces 2 and 3 illustrate some other options, which are bound to be attractive because they are a great deal cheaper (table 7-4). But if the old maxim holds that you get what you pay for (and there is no free lunch), how could either compete with the effectiveness of the base force? Is there no relationship between price and performance?

One way to find out is to take the most demanding scenario dreamt up by the Joint Staff planners and test the three forces under these difficult conditions. As it turns out, the invasion of Poland and Lithuania by Russian and Belarussian divisions makes the greatest demand on the base force when the decision is made to apply overwhelming U.S. military power. To defeat this invasion, according to the Joint Staff, entails not only a large European contingent from NATO but also virtually all the active-duty divisions in the base force, all the active Air Force fighter-attack wings, and even some reserve Air Force fighter wings, as well as two large Marine Corps air wings (table 7-5). It is the mother of all force requirements.

Table 7-4. Numbers and Annual Cost of Ground and Tactical Air Forces
Costs in billions of 1993 dollars in budget authority

	Base force		Force 2		Force 3	
Item	*Number*	*Cost*	*Number*	*Cost*	*Number*	*Cost*
Ground forces						
Active Army divisions						
Armor	2	7.0	2	7.0	. . .	. . .
Mechanized	6	20.4	3	10.2	$2\frac{1}{3}$	7.9
Airborne	1	2.8	1	2.8	1	2.8
Air assault	1	3.6	. . .	. . .	1	3.6
Light infantry	2	5.1	1	2.4	. . .	. . .
Active Army regiments						
Ranger	1	1.3	1	1.3	1	1.3
Reserve Army divisions						
Armor	3	1.8	3	1.8	3	1.8
Mechanized	2	1.3	2	1.3	2	1.3
Light infantry	1	0.5	1	0.5	1	0.5
Reserve Army brigades						
Roundout units	2	0.2	2	0.2	2	0.2
Active Marine Corps divisions	3	5.0	3	5.0	3	5.0
Reserve Marine Corps divisions	1	0.6	1	0.6	1	0.6
Subtotal	25	49.6	20	33.1	$17\frac{1}{3}$	25.0
Land-based tactical air forces					3	
Active Marine Corps air wings	3	6.8	3	6.8	1	6.8
Reserve Marine Corps air wings	1	0.6	1	0.6		0.6
Active Air Force aircraft						
B-52	68	3.4	68	3.4	68	3.4
A-10	216	2.2	216	2.2	144	1.5
F-15	216	3.6	216	3.6	144	2.4
F-111	72	1.4	72	1.4	36	0.7
F-15E	72	1.2	72	1.2	72	1.2
F-16	432	5.7	432	5.7	360	4.8
F-117A	58	1.8	58	1.8	58	1.8
RF-4	72	0.7	72	0.7	72	0.7
E-3	29	1.7	29	1.7	29	1.7
Other	900	8.0	900	8.0	405	3.6
Subtotal	2,135	29.7	2,135	29.7	1,388	21.8
Reserve Air Force aircraft						
A-10	144	0.4	144	0.4	144	0.4
F-15	288	0.2	288	0.2	288	0.2
F-16	360	1.7	360	1.7	360	1.7
RF-4	72	2.0	72	2.0	72	2.0
Subtotal	864	4.3	864	4.3	864	4.3

Sources: Author's estimates; and *Department of Defense Annual Report, Fiscal Year 1993*, pp. 69, 80, 83.

Table 7-5. Typical Marine Corps Air Wing

Aircraft	Number	Aircraft	Number
F/A-18	48	CH-46 (helicopter)	60
A-6	10	CH-53 (helicopter)	48
AV-8B	60	AH-1 (helicopter)	24
F/A-18D	12	UH-1 (helicopter)	24
EA-6B	6	OV-10	12
KC-130	12	Total	316

Source: *Department of Defense Annual Report, Fiscal Year 1993*, p. 84.

On this occasion an air campaign disables eight enemy divisions as well as a number of strategic targets. In its wake, allied forces—with 13⅔ U.S. divisions leading the attack—overwhelm the remaining Russian and Belarussian resistance in nine and a half days. Under the same conditions, force 2 takes twelve instead of nine and a half days to destroy the enemy, although it suffers more casualties in the process. And even force 3 ends up with a decisive victory, although the allied counterattack takes longer and the casualties are commensurately heavier (table 7-6).

These results should not be surprising. Force 2, for example, is able to apply as much airpower to the enemy as the base force. What is more, the Joint Staff itself admitted that a U.S. commitment of 8⅓ divisions would be "adequate," especially considering that the European allies would be committing 15⅔.[5] As it turns out, force 2 can produce nine divisions and force 3 a total of six. Given the size of the allied contingent, either addition proves more than sufficient for victory, though at an increasing price in time and casualties.

The Joint Staff also requires a substantial ground contribution from the base force for the Persian Gulf and Korean contingencies. But for reasons that are obscure it does not commit more than 10⅓ Air Force wings to what is supposedly the worst eventuality—a two-front war. South Korean ground forces are a major factor in the hypothetical war with North Korea. Consequently the outcome there is less sensitive to the size of the U.S. contribution than it is in the Gulf, where allies play a much more modest role in the coalition counterattack. Nevertheless, following major air campaigns, both force 2 and force 3 are able to produce decisive victories on these two fronts, even though force 3 is designed to deal with only one major contingency at a time (table 7-6). Moreover, both forces can be deployed more rapidly than the full air and ground complement of the base force.

Table 7-6. Comparison of Tactical Air and Ground Forces in Three Contingencies

Item	Lithuania			Persian Gulf			Korea		
	Base force	Force 2	Force 3	Base force	Force 2	Force 3	Base force	Force 2	Force 3
Air campaign									
U.S. fighter attack aircraft	2,372	2,372	2,084	528	672	528	680	800	656
Sorties per day	2,372	2,372	2,084	528	672	528	680	800	656
Effectiveness per sortie versus ground targets	.075	.075	.075	.15	.15	.15	.1	.1	.1
Length of campaign (days)	47	47	47	47	47	47	63	63	63
Total sorties flown	111,484	111,484	97,948	24,816	31,584	24,816	42,840	50,400	41,328
Targets									
Strategic	1,466	1,466	1,466	733	733	733	700	700	700
Ground force equipment	21,545	21,545	21,545	5,250	5,250	5,250	10,750	10,750	10,750
Allocation of sorties									
Strategic	14,660	14,660	14,660	7,330	7,330	7,330	7,000	7,000	7,000
Ground force equipment	96,824	96,824	83,288	17,486	24,254	17,486	35,840	43,400	34,328
Ground force targets destroyed									
Equipment	7,262	7,262	6,247	2,623	3,638	2,623	3,584	4,340	3,433
Division equivalents	8	8	7	10.5	14.6	10.5	15	18	$14\frac{1}{3}$

Ground campaign									
Divisions									
Enemy	16	16	17	10.5	6.4	10.5	30	27	$30\frac{2}{3}$
Allied	$15\frac{2}{3}$	$15\frac{2}{3}$	$15\frac{2}{3}$	$2\frac{1}{3}$	$2\frac{1}{3}$	$2\frac{1}{3}$	23	23	23
U.S.	$13\frac{2}{3}$	9	6	$5\frac{2}{3}$	$4\frac{2}{3}$	$4\frac{1}{3}$	$7\frac{1}{3}$	$4\frac{1}{3}$	3
Coalition total	$29\frac{1}{3}$	$24\frac{2}{3}$	$21\frac{2}{3}$	8	7	$6\frac{2}{3}$	$30\frac{1}{3}$	$27\frac{1}{3}$	26
Coalition combat power	43	$33\frac{2}{3}$	$27\frac{2}{3}$	24	21	20	$37\frac{2}{3}$	$31\frac{2}{3}$	29
Coalition daily effectiveness	.04	.04	.04	.12	.12	.12	.054	.05	.047
Enemy daily effectiveness	.02	.02	.02	.01	.01	.01	.02	.02	.02
Outcome									
Length of counterattack (days)	9.5	12.4	16.5	3.7	2.6	4.4	16.1	19.1	27.6
Enemy divisions surviving	. . .	. . .	. . .	. . .	. . .	. . .	. . .	. . .	. . .
Coalition divisions surviving	28.3	23.2	19.5	7.9	6.97	6.6	26.5	23.0	18.8
Casualties									
Coalition total	4,390	6,100	9,150	425	120	330	16,160	18,340	30,500
U.S. only	2,050	2,230	2,530	190	80	220	3,910	2,910	3,520
Fatalities									
Coalition total	1,100	1,520	2,290	106	30	80	4,040	4,580	7,630
U.S. only	515	560	630	50	20	50	980	730	880

Sources: Author's estimates; Patrick E. Tyler, "7 Hypothetical Conflicts Foreseen by the Pentagon," *New York Times*, February 17, 1992, p. A8; and Barton Gellman, "Pentagon War Scenario Spotlights Russia," *Washington Post*, February 20, 1992, pp. A1, A21.

Forward Presence

To facilitate its reactions to a crisis, the base force in peacetime would presumably maintain a large forward presence. It would keep two heavy divisions in Europe, along with perhaps three Air Force fighter wings, a division and four fighter squadrons in South Korea, most of a Marine expeditionary force in Okinawa, and carrier battle groups on station in the Mediterranean and the western Pacific or Arabian Sea.[6] Force 2, by contrast, would withdraw one of the divisions and four of the fighter squadrons from Europe and the division from South Korea. Carrier battle groups would be based on the east and west coasts of the United States and would cruise periodically in foreign waters. Force 3 would adopt a similar pattern of peacetime deployments (table 7-7).

Naval Comparisons

The published versions of the DPG contingencies and Joint Staff scenarios are conveniently vague about the role of the Navy in major hypothetical conflicts. Such obscurity inevitably raises the issue of whether the United States needs as much navy as is programmed in the base force. Currently the Russian fleets constitute the only serious challenge to the freedom of the seas. The Joint Staff assumes, however, that Russia would sit on the sidelines in the event of conflicts in the Persian Gulf and Korea. In the circumstances, there would not be a strong demand for ships and submarines, although the Navy managed to deploy 106 vessels to the Gulf during Desert Shield and Desert Storm.[7] It is even hard to imagine a major role for carrier battle groups in these types of conflicts in light of the availability of ample land-based airpower. However, contingencies such as a coup in the Philippines, a further confrontation with Libya, or the need to provide air cover over Bosnia—all without easy access to land bases—could justify a total of six deployable carrier battle groups. With four on station, they could provide at least 240 fighter and attack sorties a day, more than enough to remove any local air threat and attack selected targets on the ground. The amphibious lift for two Marine expeditionary brigades could also prove useful in these circumstances (table 7-8).

The Lithuanian scenario, involving as it does direct conflict with Russia, represents another problem altogether. On the one hand, it suggests not only that a major regional conflict remains possible but also that the Navy could have more on its hands than a Russian fleet in the Baltic. The Joint Staff seems to assume that such a conflict would be limited geographically. But there can be no assurance that the Russian fleets in Murmansk and Vladivostok, unless deterred, would not seek to disrupt U.S. sea lines of communication in the Atlantic and Pacific. On the other hand, since the war would be relatively short, it is not clear how disruptive they could be.

The cheapest way to deal with this problem is to negotiate naval limits on Russian and U.S. fleets. Another option is to reduce the base force to a one-ocean navy, which would require cuts in the number of attack submarines and surface combatants. A third choice is to preserve the key elements of a two-ocean navy by increasing somewhat the size of the attack submarine force over the number prescribed in the base force, maintaining the large fleet of P-3 patrol aircraft, and reducing the number of surface combatants, a step that would permit a halt to further construction of the costly DDG-51 guided missile destroyer (table 7-8). Either of these last two options would leave force 2 with a total of 260 active-duty battle force ships (counting the training carrier but not including the 18 Trident submarines and their support ships). Force 3 would support a slightly smaller fleet because it would cut the power projection component to five carrier battle groups and the amphibious lift for one Marine expeditionary brigade (table 7-8).

Budgets and Savings

Secretary Cheney has estimated that by fiscal 1997 the base force required to cover both nuclear and non-nuclear contingencies will cost $237.5 billion, in 1993 dollars.[8] This estimate allows for the reduction in strategic nuclear forces that would be brought about by the Bush-Yeltsin accord. But these savings would be offset by the funding of a single GPALS site. Force 2 budget authority, in the same dollars and for the same contingencies, would amount to $173.3 billion. The price of force 3, designed for a less threatening world, would come to $135 billion (table 7-9).

Cheney has proposed the appropriation of $1,255.3 billion, in 1993 dollars, during the coming five fiscal years.[9] How much of that could

Table 7-7. Estimated Peacetime Overseas Deployments
Personnel in thousands

Area	Base force Units	Base force Personnel	Force 2 Units	Force 2 Personnel	Force 3 Units	Force 3 Personnel
Europe and Mediterranean						
Divisions	2	70.0	1	35.0	1	35.0
Tactical air wings	3	22.5	$1\frac{2}{3}$	12.5	$1\frac{2}{3}$	12.5
Carrier battle groups	2	32.0	...	...	...	...
Marine expeditionary units	1	2.5	...	...	...	...
Northeast Asia and Indian Ocean						
Divisions	1	35.0	...	...	...	...
Marine expeditionary forces	1	42.5	1	42.5	1	42.5
Tactical air wings	$1\frac{1}{3}$	10.0	$1\frac{1}{3}$	10.0	$1\frac{1}{3}$	10.0
Carrier battle groups	2	32.0	...	...	...	...
Other	...	35.0	...	35.0	...	35.0
Total personnel	...	281.5	...	135.0	...	135.0

Sources: Author's estimates; Steven Kosiak and Paul Taibl, "Analysis of the Fiscal Year 1993 Defense Budget Request," Defense Budget Project, Washington, March 11, 1992, pp. 4–5; and *Department of Defense Annual Report, Fiscal Year 1993*, p. 136, table B-2.

Table 7-8. Three Non-Nuclear Naval Forces

Ship or aircraft	Base force	Force 2	Force 3
Aircraft carriers	13[a]	7[a]	7[a]
Surface combatants	143	60	60
Attack submarines	79	84	42
Amphibious warfare	49	31	16
Mine warfare	15	15	15
Support	96	63	45
Total	395	260	185
P-3 patrol aircraft	260	260	260

Sources: *Department of Defense Annual Report, Fiscal Year 1993*, p. 75, table 11; and author's estimates.
a. Total includes a training carrier.

be saved by moving toward force 2 or force 3 will depend on the rate at which the U.S. economy improves and future trends in world affairs. These factors, along with more parochial considerations, will largely determine the pace at which defense cuts are made and how far they go. To ease the transition from military to civilian production, Congress has already appropriated approximately $7 billion, and in future years substantially more funds could be shifted to domestic purposes, which would alleviate the economic effects of further defense reductions.[10] On the international front, concerns about an additional proliferation of nuclear weapons and advanced delivery systems could be reduced

Table 7-9. Annual Cost of Major Force Planning Contingencies
Billions of 1993 dollars in budget authority

Contingency	Base force	Force 2	Force 3
Strategic nuclear deterrence	39.3	20.5	11.2
Tactical nuclear deterrence	0.4	. . .	. . .
Non-nuclear			
Persian Gulf	47.8	36.9	29.5
Republic of Korea	59.4	31.6	24.5
Sea control	14.8	13.5	6.8
Panama	8.6	10.0	8.5
Philippines	13.6	9.6	7.5
Not deployed	20.0	17.6	13.4
Airlift-sealift	13.7	13.7	13.7
National intelligence and			
communications	19.9	19.9	19.9
Total	237.5	173.3	135.0

Sources: Tyler, "7 Hypothetical Conflicts Foreseen by the Pentagon," p. A8; Gellman, "Pentagon War Scenario Spotlights Russia"; and author's estimates.

through a number of U.S. and allied measures. There is also the possibility that Russia will continue on the path to democracy and a more market-oriented economy, that the United Nations will put a permanent damper on Iraqi ambitions, and that North Korea will give up any designs it may have on South Korea. Indeed, should this turn out to be the wave of the future, the authors of the DPG will find it difficult to replace expected threats with anything of comparable menace and plausibility, unless China begins to develop an imperial appetite.

But the future may still prove to be at least as ominous as the DPG and the Joint Staff foresee, despite efforts by the United States and its allies to shape the course of events. Such a possibility may persuade the interested purchaser of defense that the base force remains the best hedge against an uncertain future. There is, however, another choice—to buy time and defer any radical cuts until better information is available. Starting in fiscal 1993 the path toward force 2 can be maintained while keeping open the freedom to halt the journey before fiscal 1997 if international relations deteriorate. After 1997, if the news remains good, force 2 can proceed to force 3, with reasonable confidence that the country will be no less secure with force 2 or force 3 than with the overdesigned and underutilized base force. The reward for this caution would be a five-year real saving in budget authority of $183 billion and a ten-year saving of $623 billion. Savings in outlays would be slightly lower over the ten-year period (table 7-10). These amounts, it should be added, are based on estimated budget authority and outlays for the Defense Department. If reductions are also made in the budget for the military applications of atomic energy (currently in the Energy Department) to allow for an end to nuclear weapons tests and the deferral of new production of tritium, additional savings in national defense over the five-year period could amount to $15.6 billion in budget authority and $14.9 billion in outlays—all in 1993 dollars (table 7-11).

Both force 2 and force 3 would have sufficient resources to provide enough well-trained personnel for the efficient operational support of all combat capabilities. Maintenance, readiness, and war reserve stocks would remain high. Modernization would also continue, based on a policy of upgrading existing equipment, fostering research and development, and selectively replacing older weapons when efficiency or the competition demands it (table 7-12). The same cannot be said

Table 7-10. Alternative Ten-Year Plans for the Defense Department,
Fiscal Years 1993–2002
Billions of 1993 dollars

Year	Base force	Force 2 and force 3	Annual difference	Cumulative difference
1993	267.6	260.0	7.6	7.6
1994	258.0	234.9	23.1	30.7
1995	250.4	212.3	38.1	68.8
1996	241.8	191.8	50.0	118.8
1997	237.5	173.3	64.2	183.0
Five-year total (051)				
Budget authority	1,255.3	1,072.3	. . .	183.0
Outlays	1,257.4	1,074.1	. . .	183.3
1998	237.5	164.9	72.6	255.6
1999	237.5	156.8	80.7	336.3
2000	237.5	149.2	88.3	424.6
2001	237.5	141.9	95.6	520.2
2002	237.5	135.0	102.5	622.7
Ten-year total (051)	-			
Budget authority	2,442.8	1,820.1	. . .	622.7
Outlays	2,439.9	1,817.9	. . .	622.0

Sources: *Department of Defense Annual Report, Fiscal Year 1993*, pp. 21–22; and author's estimates.

with confidence about the base force. Because so many new systems in the investment pipeline are moving toward procurement, despite Cheney's many cancellations and deferrals, additional funds will be needed by the late 1990s to acquire, operate, and support them. Inevitably, the base force will have to shrink further, more systems such as the F-22 stealth fighter and GPALS will have to be killed, or defense budgets will have to increase in real terms. At a minimum, a "buyer beware" sticker needs to be attached to the base force.

Choices

The original draft of the DPG represented the professional pessimist's assessment of the new world order and a very conservative view of its implications for U.S. military power. Perhaps intentionally, the revised draft has sounded a more optimistic note. It makes the suggestion that a leveling of military investment coupled with greater cooperation for economic and military security will create a more stable world, and it describes the United States as seeking to "provide security at lower costs and with lower risks for all." It also refers to

Table 7-11. Alternative Five-Year Plans for National Defense, Fiscal Years 1993–97
Billions of 1993 dollars

Item	1993	1994	1995	1996	1997	Total
Budget authority						
Base force	280.9	271.4	263.9	255.5	251.3	1,323.0
Forces 2 and 3	272.3	246.2	222.6	201.3	182.0	1,124.4
Annual reduction	8.6	25.2	41.3	54.2	69.3	. . .
Cumulative reduction	8.6	33.8	75.1	129.3	198.6	198.6
Outlays						
Base force	285.9	270.7	261.5	255.4	249.9	1,323.4
Forces 2 and 3	276.7	245.6	220.7	201.2	181.0	1,125.2
Annual reduction	9.2	25.1	40.8	54.2	68.9	. . .
Cumulative reduction	9.2	34.3	75.1	129.3	198.2	198.2

Sources: *Department of Defense Annual Report, Fiscal Year 1993*, p. 21, table 3; and author's estimates.

tools that "include political and economic measures and others such as security assistance, military-to-military contacts, humanitarian aid and intelligence assistance, as well as security measures to prevent the emergence of a non-democratic aggressor in critical regions." And the new draft predicts that in "this more secure international environment, there will be enhanced opportunities for political, economic, environmental, social and security issues to be resolved through new or revitalized international organizations, including the United Nations, or regional arrangements."[11] Strangely enough, however, this relatively optimistic vision of the future failed to affect the contingencies and strategy of the earlier draft.

Table 7-12. Breakdown of Costs, by Appropriation Title
Billions of 1993 dollars in budget authority

Appropriation title	Base force	Force 2	Force 3
Military personnel	64.0	47.1	38.9
Operations and maintenance	77.8	52.8	43.6
Procurement	55.6	42.6	27.4
Research, development, test, and evaluation	31.6	25.1	20.4
Military construction	4.8	3.5	3.0
Family housing	3.2	2.0	1.5
Other	0.5	0.2	0.2
Total	237.5	173.3	135.0
Investment subtotal	92.0	71.2	50.8
Operating and support subtotal	145.5	102.1	84.2

Source: Keith Berner and Stephen Daggett, "Defense Budget for FY 1993: Data Summary," CRS Report to Congress, 92-162F, Congressional Research Service, Washington, March 18, 1992, table VIII, p. 15; and author's estimates.

That is unfortunate. What is by all accounts a more sophisticated and less academically trendy discussion of the basis for national security planning might have offered an alternative to the assumptions that managed to produce the base force. At most, however, the Russian foray into Poland and Lithuania has been dropped from the menu of force planning contingencies. Meanwhile the base force goes on, apparently insensitive to everything but the internal dynamics of the Pentagon. Sadly enough, George Santayana may have had it right when he wrote, "The working of great institutions is mainly the result of a vast mass of routine, petty malice, self interest, carelessness, and sheer mistake. Only a residual fraction is thought." Still, as Winston S. Churchill once observed, "You cannot ask us to take sides against arithmetic. You cannot ask us to take sides against the obvious facts of the situation." Choices are still possible. To govern is to choose.

Notes

1. *Department of Defense Annual Report, Fiscal Year 1993*, p. ix.
2. Ibid., p. 65.
3. Barton Gellman, "Pentagon War Scenario Spotlights Russia," *Washington Post*, February 20, 1992, p. A21.
4. Bob Woodward, *The Commanders* (Simon and Schuster, 1991), p. 249.
5. Gellman, "Pentagon War Scenario Spotlights Russia," p. A21.
6. Steven Kosiak and Paul Taibl, "Analysis of the Fiscal Year 1993 Defense Budget Request," Defense Budget Project, Washington, March 11, 1992, pp. 4–5.
7. *Department of Defense Annual Report, Fiscal Year 1993*, p. 75.
8. Ibid., p. 22.
9. Ibid.
10. Louis Uchitelle, "Cutback in Military Spending: No Help for Ailing Economy," *New York Times*, August 12, 1992, pp. A1, D2.
11. Quoted in Patrick E. Tyler, "Pentagon Drops Goal of Blocking New Superpowers," *New York Times*, May 24, 1992, p. 14.

APPENDIX

THE TEXT CONTAINS tables of numerical data that measure the outcomes of Desert Storm and hypothetical military campaigns in the Persian Gulf, Korea, and Eastern Europe.[1] These results should not be mistaken for predictions of future wars or their outcomes. The numbers displayed in various tables and discussed in the text come from the interaction of only a few variables. Moreover, these variables reflect almost exclusively the material capabilities of U.S., allied, and enemy forces.

The non-nuclear conflicts analyzed assumed two basic scenarios: one in which an allied air campaign against a number of targets, including a major effort against enemy ground forces, preceded an attack by U.S. and allied ground forces (following the Desert Storm model); the other in which an allied air campaign took place but did not affect enemy troop strength, so that the subsequent allied ground attack encountered an unweakened enemy.

The air campaigns that followed the Desert Storm model assumed that the United States and its allies won air supremacy without any significant loss to the enemy. During this phase and subsequently, they attacked a mixture of strategic and tactical targets. An average kill probability was assigned regardless of the type of target, aircraft, or munition, partly for the sake of simplicity, and partly to calibrate the results with those of Desert Storm. Each aircraft flew one sortie a day. Strategic targets, defined as everything but ground forces, were allocated ten sorties each. All remaining sorties were allocated to tactical targets, namely enemy tanks, artillery pieces, and armored personnel vehicles.

The kill probability of .15 assigned to allied aircraft in their attacks on Iraqi ground forces is consistent with the results of the Desert Storm air campaign. In table 7-6, this probability was lowered to .1 in the Korean case, and to .075 in the campaign in Eastern Europe, to reflect differences in terrain, weather, and enemy countermeasures. Neither of these probabilities is grounded in experience. Each could be higher or lower. The number of aircraft and the number of sorties by each aircraft could also be varied.

The results of the ground campaigns came from the use of four equations derived from the original Lanchester formulation. The first two give the residual combat power of each combatant as a function of the amount of time spent in the ground campaign. The third postulates a battle of annihilation in which the enemy is reduced to zero forces. Its output is the percentage of the combat power of the winner surviving at the end of the fight. The fourth equation provides the amount of time taken to complete the battle of annihilation.[2] Losses expressed in divisions, casualties, and fatalities, can be deduced from the outputs of the first three equations.

Each equation requires the input of the combat power and daily effectiveness of each side at the start of the ground campaign. The first two equations also require the number of days spent from the start of the campaign. Elaborate scoring methods were avoided in determining the combat power of the forces. Enemy divisions were simply counted; each U.S. and allied division was rated as equal to or more numerous than that of the enemy by a factor of two or more. The equations themselves were used to determine the combat power and daily effectiveness of the forces not only in Desert Storm, but also in the hypothetical Persian Gulf, Korean, and East European contingencies. It became difficult, in the process of doing so, to reconcile moderately effective air campaigns and plausible performance by U.S., allied, and enemy ground forces with the length of time deemed necessary by the Joint Staff to gain a decisive victory over the enemy in each of these cases.

The four equations used in these analyses are

$$B_t = \left[\left(B - \frac{r^{1/2}}{b^{1/2}} R \right) e^{(rb)^{1/2} t} + \left(B + \frac{r^{1/2}}{b^{1/2}} R \right) e^{-(rb)^{1/2} t} \right] .5$$

$$R_t = \left[\left(R - \frac{b^{1/2}}{r^{1/2}} B \right) e^{(rb)^{1/2} t} + \left(R + \frac{b^{1/2}}{r^{1/2}} B \right) e^{-(rb)^{1/2} t} \right] .5$$

$$B_{end} = \left(1 - \frac{R^2 r}{B^2 b} \right)^{1/2}$$

$$t_{end} = \frac{1}{(rb)^{1/2}} \ln \left[\frac{(B^2b)^{1/2} + (R^2r)^{1/2}}{(B^2b)^{1/2} - (R^2r)^{1/2}} \right]^{1/2},$$

where:

B = allied ground combat power
R = enemy ground combat power
b = allied daily effectiveness
r = enemy daily effectiveness
t = number of days from the start of the ground campaign.

A simulation of the Desert Storm ground battle will illustrate the types of assumptions made and the operation of the equations. In the first two equations, 4 allied and 8 U.S. divisions are considered to be worth the equivalent of 36 Iraqi divisions in combat power and to have a daily effectiveness of .12. Iraqi ground forces are reduced by the air campaign from 42 to 21 divisions with a daily effectiveness of .01.

Surviving allied forces after 100 hours, or 4.1667 days, of ground combat would be

$$B_t = \left[\left(36 - \frac{.01^{1/2}}{.12^{1/2}} 21 \right) e^{(.01 \times .12)^{1/2} \times 4.1667} \right.$$

$$\left. + \left(36 + \frac{.01^{1/2}}{.12^{1/2}} 21 \right) e^{-(.01 \times .12)^{1/2} \times 4.1667} \right] .5 = 35.4976.$$

Surviving allied divisions $= \dfrac{35.4976}{36} \times 12 = 11.8325$

Allied casualties $= (12 - 11.8325) \times 17,000 \times .25 = 712$
Allied fatalities $= 712 \times .25 = 178$

U.S. casualties $= 712 \times \dfrac{8}{12} = 475$

U.S. fatalities $= 475 \times .25 = 119.$

Surviving Iraqi divisions after 4.1667 days of ground combat would be

$$R_t = \left[\left(21 - \frac{.12^{1/2}}{.01^{1/2}} 36 \right) e^{(.01 \times .12)^{1/2} \times 4.1667} \right.$$

$$\left. + \left(21 + \frac{.12^{1/2}}{.01^{1/2}} 36 \right) e^{-(.01 \times .12)^{1/2} \times 4.1667} \right] .5 = 3.16.$$

Surviving Iraqi personnel = $3.16 \times 8,667 = 27,388$ (who presumably fled north).

Iraqi killed, wounded, captured = $154,612$ (in addition to those lost during the air campaign).

If Desert Storm had resulted in a battle of annihilation and reduced Iraqi forces to zero active combatants, surviving allied ground forces would have been:

$$B_{end} = \left(1 - \frac{21^2 \times .01}{36^2 \times .12}\right)^{1/2} = .9857$$

$$.9857 \times 12 = 11.8286.$$

Time to fight the battle of annihilation would have been

$$t_{end(days)} = \frac{1}{(.01 \times .12)^{1/2}} \ln \left[\frac{(36^2 \times .12)^{1/2} + (21^2 \times .01)^{1/2}}{(36^2 \times .12)^{1/2} - (21^2 \times .01)^{1/2}}\right]^{1/2} = 4.9079.$$

In other words, a battle of annihilation would have taken approximately 18 more hours and resulted in 17 more allied casualties, 11 of which would have been from the United States. Thus

Additional hours = $(4.9079 \times 24) - (4.1667 \times 24) = 17.8$

Additional allied casualties = $11.8325 - 11.8286 = .0039$

$\qquad .0039 \times 17,000 \times .25 = 16.6$

Additional U.S. casualties = $16.6 \times .6667 = 11.1$.

Notes to Appendix

1. See tables 6-3, 6-4, 6-5, 6-6, 6-7, and 7-6.

2. The equations are from Yu. V. Chuyev and Yu. B. Mikhaylov, *Forecasting in Military Affairs: A Soviet View* (Washington: Government Printing Office, 1980). The original Lanchester formulation is most easily accessible in Frederick William Lanchester, "Mathematics in Warfare," in James R. Newman, *The World of Mathematics* (Simon and Schuster, 1956), vol. 4, pp. 2138–57.